COYOTEWAY

Twelve Additional Photographs
from Archival Sources
Ceremonial Photographs and Other Illustrations
by the Author

COYOTEWAY

a Navajo Holyway Healing Ceremonial

KARL W. LUCKERT
Johnny C. Cooke, Navajo Interpreter

With additional texts by
Mary C. Wheelwright, Maud Oakes, and others

The University of Arizona Press / Tucson
and the
Museum of Northern Arizona Press / Flagstaff

About the Author . : .

Karl W. Luckert has maintained a continuing interest in the fields of philosophy and religion. After receiving a Ph.D. in the history of religions at the University of Chicago, in 1969, he accepted a teaching position in the humanities at Northern Arizona University. In 1977 Luckert founded and became general editor of the "American Tribal Religions" monograph series. Author Luckert's published works include *The Navajo Hunter Tradition, Olmec Religion, Navajo Mountain and Rainbow Bridge Religion,* and *A Navajo Bringing-Home Ceremony.*

970.3
N31lu

THE UNIVERSITY OF ARIZONA PRESS & THE MUSEUM OF NORTHERN ARIZONA
CO-PUBLISHERS
Copyright███████ for both agencies 1979
The Arizona Board of Regents (for the Press) & the Museum of Northern Arizona
All Rights Reserved
Manufactured in the U.S.A.

Library of Congress Cataloging in Publication Data

Luckert, Karl W.   1934–
    Coyoteway.

    Bibliography: p.
    Includes index.
    1. Navaho Indians—Rites and ceremonies. 2. Navaho
Indians—Medicine. 3. Indians of North America—
Southwest, New—Rites and ceremonies. 4. Indians of
North America—Southwest, New—Medicine. I. Title.
E99.N3L8 1978   392   78-10358
ISBN 0-8165-0670-1
ISBN 0-8165-0655-8 pbk. 80-9883

[iv]

Contents

[v]

Charts

Illustrations

Preface

Three men, especially, deserve the gratitude of writer, reader, and posterity; they are Johnny C. Cooke (John Cook), Luke Cook, and Man With Palomino Horse. Johnny Cooke has been my faithful interpreter through three major research projects. His superior command of the Navajo language and his open-minded religious sensitivity have been the key to success in both our negotiations and in the translation of the materials. A sincere word of thanks is hereby also extended to his wife and children for enduring his frequent absences from home. Luke Cook has been a devoted negotiator on our behalf, later also a very helpful informant. He has selflessly volunteered to be our patient, and, seeing himself in the traditional way still as the primary beneficiary, he has insisted on bearing certain portions of the expenses himself. The consent of his family, and the active support of his family, his relatives and friends, is forever appreciated. Man With Palomino Horse, one of two surviving singers of Coyoteway (mạ'iijí hatáál), has consented to have his chantway recorded and preserved for posterity. Many generations of Navajo students and world citizens will admire him for his generous gesture toward a closed future. The world will never know the struggle that went on behind his serene and dignified posture. Should Coyoteway die ethnically pure, or should it be given to mankind? Some people despair when they face the end of a road; Man With Palomino Horse dreamt a broader vision.

A number of other people have helped me along the way. Melvin Nelson, of Winslow, on many occasions during the negotiation stage, has saved me many miles of extra driving by keeping our "pony express" relay communications system going. When the ceremonial finally got off the ground, it was my Northern Arizona University colleague, Bill Gillette, who let me use his professional flash equipment to improve my photography. Then, in the days after winter recess, when it appears to be difficult to grant leaves of absence in Arizona, the Northern Arizona University administration graciously gave me two additional days. Irvy W. Goossen, another university colleague and professor of Navajo, has helped me over and again with transcribing Navajo words. His transcriptions correspond to the Young and Morgan orthography. Barton Wright has discussed comparative Hopi materials with me, and the library staff at the Museum of Northern Arizona has been as generous toward me as always. Sam Gill, formerly a fellow student at the University of Chicago, has through his work on Navajo prayer been a stimulus for many an inspiration.

Before the manuscript was given to the University of Arizona Press, two anthropologists with expertise in the Apachean field, Leland C. Wyman and Morris E. Opler, together with a historian of religions, Benjamin Ray, graciously consented to read it. The book owes many improvements to their informed suggestions. It is difficult to estimate the large debt which this author owes to the work of these and other scholars. Without their generous assistance this publication would not have had a chance to become what it now is. The many shortcomings which will undoubtedly be found when I look at it ten years from now must not be charged to the advice of others but to my own limited horizon.

While the greater portion of the expenses for this project has been paid by myself—and suffered wonderingly by my family—two partial grants-in-aid eventually came my way: one from the Smithsonian Institution and another from the Wenner-Gren Foundation. Then, in the summer of 1974, while working on the manuscript, I was given five weeks of support from Northern Arizona University. To all these institutions I express my sincerest appreciation.

Chapters 9 through 12 in this book contain materials which have been archived in the Museum of Navaho Ceremonial Art, Inc., at Santa Fe. Director Bertha Dutton and Curator of Archives Caroline Olin have supplied me with manuscripts of unpublished Coyoteway myths; they have provided photo prints of thirteen Coyoteway sand-paintings; and they have graciously mediated and granted permission to print. Maud Oakes has given permission to include her Coyoteway myth by William Charlie. Without the dedicated work done through time by people associated with this and other museums, we would all know less about Coyoteway than we now do.

*   *   *

After a number of years have passed over a printed report of this kind, attitudes and theories in the fields of history of religions and anthropology will undoubtedly have changed. One can expect that readers will want to question my materials in relation to my methods and procedures. Since personal ambitions and attitudes are inseparable from methodology, I have decided to provide readers with at least a hint of how Coyoteway was found and experienced by me. The possibility that such a statement will be judged as self-serving dwindles in the face of the greater likelihood that future readers, who have outgrown the mistakes of my generation, will on the basis of these disclosures find me quite inadequate. Yet, in fairness to Coyoteway and to future generations of students, I think that this risk should be taken.

My first knowledge about the presence of Coyoteway on the Navajo Reservation I owe to two scholars, Jerrold Levy, a professor of anthropology from Portland, Oregon, and Oswald Werner, a professor of linguistics from Evanston, Illinois. Both men were interested in recording as much as possible of the Coyoteway tradition. They were in touch with a Coyoteway singer somewhere on Black Mesa, though this happened not to be the singer with whom I eventually worked.

One year later, in the summer of 1971, I traveled into the field in search of materials related to the Navajo hunter tradition. Johnny Cooke, a Presbyterian theology student from Chinle, was my Navajo interpreter. During one of our numerous trips we visited Johnny's parental home at Black Mesa. We had come to put earmarkers on some steers and calves. After wrestling these animals, we offered to play tapes of a Navajo hunter myth to Luke Cook, Johnny's father.

That meeting marked the beginning of a developing friendship with the Cook family—in time I became known there affectionately as Johnny's Grandfather. A comparison of Navajo and Israelite religion helped unexpectedly to build a bridge of understanding between the traditional father and his seemingly estranged Christian son. The Navajo Deerway myth (Luckert 1975) was easily grasped by both men as a pre-pastoralist, and thus a type of pre-Abrahamic, revelation of God Almighty. To both it became clear that the God, whom nobody has managed to describe accurately thus far, has revealed himself to Navajo hunter ancestors, among other manifestations, in the form of sacrificial Deer People. As a Lamb he seems to have shown himself to Hebrew shepherds, eventually also as an anthropomorphic savior. Luke Cook was quick to see that this same God could also have appeared as Coyote.

When father and son found similarities in these two traditions, it was definitely not the result of persuasion on my part. Rather, it was the kind of natural synthesis which rational people in all cultures have been making all along, especially when they were faced with having to live concurrently in two cultures. The fact that we all live in the same world necessitates that we share with one another our hypotheses and axioms. Moreover, in all my contacts with Navajo singers I have not met one who would have found it difficult to think of his gods collectively as a single supreme personage—in terms of monotheism.

On that occasion Luke Cook told us about two Coyoteway singers who were still alive and able to perform. Both lived somewhere in the southern portion of Black Mesa. On later occasions I was told that some years before, Luke Cook himself had been an apprentice to a Coyoteway singer. By now his family had been converted to Christianity and he had ceased to help in the traditional ceremonials. A gradual change of attitude toward us could be observed when Luke Cook sensed his son's new interest in his traditional ways. This is why he gradually began to confide to us a few points of general information about the Coyoteway ceremonial. As an apprentice who had ceased helping in the ceremonials he did not feel authorized to give us specific songs, prayers, or stories.

In January 1973, Johnny Cooke and I drove to Black Mesa and found our Coyoteway singer, Man With Palomino Horse. Would he tell us the Coyoteway myth and sing the songs for us? His answer at first was no. But then, when Johnny introduced himself as the son of Luke Cook (chishi biye'), the practitioner began to take us more seriously. All along he had been doubting our sincerity. His foremost concern now was that he was getting old and that he had no apprentice to carry on the Coyoteway tradition. No doubt this was an oblique reference to Luke Cook's terminated apprenticeship. We told him straightforwardly that as Christians we could not become his apprentices, but that we respected and would like to record his chantway in order to preserve it in a book for future generations. Perhaps someday in the future, after we had all gone the paths of our ancestors, young Navajo people would want to learn about this tradition. This took some thinking. At last, perhaps as a favor to Luke Cook, whom he still respected and who recently had referred a patient to him, the singer agreed to have us record the Coyoteway ceremonial. Nevertheless, Coyoteway information could not be discussed and Coyote songs could not be sung apart from an actual ceremonial. We needed a patient. As we left the singer that night he suggested to us, completely on his own, that for the ceremonial we should bring a camera—there would be sandpaintings.

After midnight, through deep snow, we arrived at Luke Cook's house and told him about our meeting with Man With Palomino Horse. He was enthusiastic. Yes, the Coyoteway should be saved from complete extinction, if not by an apprentice then at least in a book. He volunteered to discuss our plans with a prospective patient he knew and to make the arrangements for us. He would then ride on horseback to the nearest telephone.

In March 1973, while doing work at the University of Oklahoma, I drove again into Navajoland to investigate. Johnny had, meanwhile, become the minister of the mission at Indian Wells; I found him there. The news he had was discouraging indeed: the shepherds around Black Mesa had suffered extensive livestock losses because of the heavy snow, and our prospective patient had died without having the benefit of a Coyoteway ceremonial. That night I fled a traffic-choking blizzard over northern Arizona and drove into the valley of Tucson; I was forced to return to Oklahoma by way of Texas.

In May we made another attempt to reach the singer. This time Luke Cook accompanied us. The proposed brief visit with the singer turned into a daylong search, one hundred miles over roads which were not roads. Our clutch gave out and had to be mended temporarily, in the midst of a sandstorm. I had to agree with my Navajo friends that "chasing a coyote is not easy." In the evening we found our man at his home. I had to agree again. "Coyote is tricky!" But if Coyote is a trickster, he also has a human heart. Our daylong ordeal of trying to find the singer convinced him of our earnest determination. It, in part, atoned the practitioner's former apprentice for not completing his apprenticeship.

At that meeting I was given a choice: either to record five nights of Coyoteway in about a week in the home of one of the singer's relatives, or to wait until a full nine-night ceremonial could be arranged. This was a difficult choice. Should I opt for the first half of the ceremonial, would I ever get the remainder? The second portion is performed only over persons who have had the first part. If I chose to wait, would a patient ever be found who needed the full nine nights? Would the singer live long enough? I decided to wait until a full nine-night performance could be arranged.

This decision became considerably easier to live with when Luke Cook disclosed some of his thoughts to me. There was an uncle, who, like himself, a former apprentice, was also eligible to have the full nine-night ceremonial performed over him as an initiatory procedure. This idea immediately appealed to me. The chance for having a full ceremonial is far greater with a patient who is to be initiated as a singer. Such a person needs the full ceremonial for his full authorization; on the other hand, if the ceremonial is performed over a patient with actual symptoms of Coyote illness, and if in the process the symptoms get worse, the performance has to stop.

My choice was rewarded with Luke Cook's further suggestion: "If this uncle will not be our patient, I myself will be it." I was elated. Now it could only be a matter of time. No ceremonial could be sponsored by the Cook family right then for two reasons. A grandmother was about to die; if that should happen the ceremony would have to stop a full month. Then, they all had suffered far too heavy livestock losses in this winter's snow. The material means for such a ceremonial were not available. As it turned out, the uncle was willing, but his family vetoed his plans for having his initiation ceremonial. It was now Luke Cook's turn to become our patient.

The final arrangements for the ceremonial required eight more months. Luke Cook decided that he should build a new hogan for the occasion. Then, we attempted to arrange a leave of absence for Johnny from his congregation. Soon it became apparent that Christ and Coyote are divine savior manifestations from widely separate culture strata. Savior figures from the hunting era and from a monarchal civilization are not as easily reconciled as some well-meaning historian of religions might think. After six more negotiation journeys to the reservation it was agreed that I would do the recording alone, and that Johnny would be free to translate from the tapes.

On the morning of January 3, 1974, the coldest and snowiest day of winter, I loaded several boxes of equipment into my vehicle and drove to Black Mesa. Beautiful snow, which at many places lay two feet deep, had to be driven through with four-wheel-drive gear, snow tires, chains, a "sheepherder's" jack, and a shovel. A severe cold began to affect me from the beginning. Three bottles of cough syrup and one bottle of antibiotics later, on January 12, I drove home. What I had experienced in these ten days belongs among the most cherished memories of my professional life. The Coyoteway ceremonial which required one year of final negotiations, five months of preparations, 15,000 miles of driving and other things, is saved from oblivion.

*   *   *

A few years later, as the manuscript approaches final preparation for becoming a book, a postscript to this Preface seems called for. Our patient, Luke Cook, participated earnestly *as if* he were to become a Coyote-priest. His participation in the Coyote ceremonial, however, was a farewell gesture to a tradition which he still respects, but which he nevertheless decided to abandon. He knows that because of his quitting, the Coyote ceremonial will become extinct in a few years. In view of this fate, he volunteered and enthusiastically cooperated in the recording procedures. The temporarily initiated Coyote-priest continues nevertheless to move closer toward Christianity.

Sentiments of lament, bordering occasionally even on hostility toward representatives of intruding religions, have been expressed by some scientific field researchers and historians of religions. Their fields have been altered before their eyes and have disappeared. And yet, life still is motion; it seldom stays fixed long enough for scientific verification. Even students of eternal things must learn to adjust to life's onward flow and learn to celebrate its passing moments. Our Coyote-way heir has as much right as any human being to follow the brightest star which he happens to see. For him Coyote has now trotted into the shadows to hide. And for the historical record it must be said that, at this point in time, his guiding light and divine tutelary is Christ. The process of divine revelation does not stop just because a Coyote hides in the bushes.

K. W. L.

PART ONE:

THE CEREMONIAL
AND ITS PRIESTS

Introduction to Coyoteway

Navajo religion consists of twenty or more overlapping but nevertheless distinct ceremonial traditions. In the opinion of this writer these traditions are traceable in mythology, by way of geographized ecstatic journeys (vision quests), to their respective shamanic founder or founders. They are traceable in history, possibly, to a point in time when several formerly shamanic traditions became amalgamated into the conglomerate healing ceremonials of later priestly *hataałii* or "singers." Since my general views on Navajo religious history have recently been published (Luckert 1975), this statement on the subject of historical development is brief.

The arrival of the first Navajo-Apachean hunters in the Southwest, from the north, is commonly estimated at about A.D. 1500. In the sixteenth and seventeenth centuries most of the healing rituals of the Navajo-Apacheans were probably still securely anchored in hunter ideology. But after coming to the Southwest, and after a change in life-style, their hunting and their hunting rites became less important. At the same time, the direct concern for health in ceremonialism remained. In dialogue and in competition with representatives of Pueblo Indian maize-planter cultures, the Navajo-Apachean hunter shaman, with his northern Athapascan heritage, has gradually adapted to become a sort of learned professional—a priestly performer of composite song-ceremonials, thus a "singer."

Pueblo Indian cosmology, the world view which has been taking shape in the Southwest for about two thousand years, appears to be in its basic outline a product of the great archaic civilization of Middle America (see Luckert 1976). Its basic notions are explained in terms of prehuman events in the myth of emergence. For instance, according to Hopi tradition, the mythic evolutionary emergence of the people from the underworld is generally divided into four stages. The "fourth world" of present-day earth-surface people is again structured numerically in relation to four cardinal points. Specialized gods preside over each of the four directions.

Confronted by this tightly structured view of a planter people's universe, the early Navajo-Apachean shaman found himself groping for answers which would relate his divine hunter tutelaries to the directionally stationed gods of the Southwest. For the traditionally individualistic shaman it was no longer sufficient to encounter one divine guardian at a time, or to get initiated by a predecessor into a close relationship with that divine guardian. Confronted by Pueblo Indian systematic cosmology he needed the combined strength of his Athapascan heritage to achieve a synthesis that would fall short of total surrender. And so it seems that Navajo narrators of myths began to draw increasingly from a larger number of available shamanic formulations. As scholastic syntheses, the originally shamanic bodies of knowledge ceased to be shamanic. Instantaneous communication with divine tutelaries was replaced increasingly by systematic learning and poetic creativity. The credit for all this creativity was, nevertheless, given to the gods, in a posture of religious humility.

While Navajo singer apprentices learned the traditions of several shamanic masters, the divine guardians of the latter assembled above them into some sort of corresponding pantheon. The result is that Navajo ceremonial traditions feature now overlapping but, nevertheless, different pantheons. And, in accordance with the four-directional scheme of Pueblo Indian cosmology, some freely roaming tutelaries of the Navajo-Apachean hunters were stationed permanently. Learned Apachean hunter lore could thus be harmonized with the priestly concepts of Pueblo Indian cosmology and anthropogony. The arrangement which has the Talking-god (haashch'éélti'í) in the east, Calling-god (haashch'éoghan) in the south, Begochidi in the west, and Black-god (haashch'ééshzhini) in the north, appears to be the most popular synthesis in the Black Mesa area. Other traditions list Calling-god as a "Talking-god in the west." Still other arrangements have a Talking-god stationed in each of the four directions, or as four divine persons in the east, or everywhere. From a historical perspective it seems that Talking-god, as an anthropomorphic "talker" associated predominantly with the White East, has risen to highest prominence.

This era of general synthesis and poetic creativity in the history of Navajo religion seems, in all likelihood, to have been precipitated by the Pueblo Revolt of 1680. Large numbers of Pueblo Indians fled from along the Rio Grande when the Spanish retaliated. Many of them were absorbed by the Navajo tribe. The stories of shamanic vision quests, brought from the north and now challenged by Pueblo cosmology and ceremonialism, were retold by fascinated newcomers in the hauntingly bright and magnificent landscape of the Southwest. All this together, in the course of a few centuries, produced a ceremonial ferment which is unequalled anywhere in North America. The challenge which is put on the priest and the mythmaker is great indeed in the Southwest, because world-sketches of heroes and gods must excel those attainable by ordinary Earth-surface people. The general pattern of this Apachean-Pueblo synthesis is still very much in evidence in the form and content (i.e., first half versus second half) of the Coyoteway ceremonial. Specifically, in this instance, this synthesis may be as recent as the early part of the nineteenth century.

According to Leland C. Wyman (1970b, p. 3), there were formerly "about twenty-three Holyway chantway systems, all for curing illnesses, to which—by elaboration according to male and female branches, ritual, and other considerations—about forty names for song ceremonials could be ascribed." Wyman's newest, at the moment

The Holyway Chantways

Shooting Chant subgroup
    Hailway *
    Waterway *
    Shootingway
    Red Antway
    Big Starway
    Flintway (?)

Mountain Chant subgroup
    Mountainway
    Beautyway
    Excessway *
    Mothway *

God-Impersonators subgroup
    Nightway
    Big Godway *
    Plumeway
    Coyoteway *
    Dogway *
    Ravenway *

Wind Chant subgroup
    Navajo Windway
    Chiricahua Windway

Hand-Trembling Chant subgroup
    Hand-Tremblingway

Eagle Trapping subgroup
    Eagleway *
    Beadway *

Extinct ceremonials of uncertain affiliation
    Awlway *
    Earthway *
    Reared-in-Earthway (?) *

* extinct, obsolescent, or virtually obsolescent.
(?) indicates questionable classification.

still unpublished, chart of these chantway systems is included here with his permission. Coyoteway is classified as a chantway of the God-Impersonators subgroup and as "virtually obsolescent."

Classification of Navajo chantways is made difficult by the fact that two somewhat independent criteria are being used interchangeably—modes of performance and etiological factors. Coyoteway is readily, and for obvious reasons, assigned to the God-Impersonators subgroup. God-impersonators do indeed appear during performance of this ceremonial. Nevertheless, based on Navajo etiological reasoning, a good case can be made for having Coyoteway in the Mountain Chant subgroup alongside *ajiłee*, the so-called Excessway.

Recent research in the *ajiłee* tradition has revealed that, rooted in the hunter tradition, Coyoteway and *ajiłee* are indeed closely related. A more extensive discussion of the *ajiłee-mą'iiji* dichotomy will have to be postponed to a forthcoming publication. Let it suffice to say here, that Luke Cook, our Coyoteway patient, has traced all illness among humankind to the great Coyote beyond the east. From there illness is conveyed to us by Sun and Moon. According to its more specific etiology, Coyote illness is mediated from Sun and Moon to humankind by predators. "It is gotten when members of the Coyote family (which in a broad sense includes all predators) put their heads together and decide to get to you." *Ajiłee* is basically the same kind of illness. It, too, is sent into our world by the great Coyote beyond the homes of Sun and Moon in the east. It, too, is conveyed into our world by these celestial personages. But in contrast to what is specifically referred to as Coyote illness, *ajiłee* is passed on to humans when they eat the meat of the game animals without the proper counter measures; it has gotten into the game animals when, in self-defense, they ate certain poisonous or hallucinogenic plants; such plants have, in turn, received *ajiłee* power from having been made pregnant by Sun and Moon.

Regardless of the subgroup to which it belongs, Coyoteway is a healing ceremonial of the Holyway type. This means, it seeks to remedy the patient's estrangement from the Holy People and his provocations toward them.[1] Angered gods, in this instance angered Coyote People, inflict their brand of illness on the human offender. Subsequently, the divine cause and his human victim must be reconciled ceremonially with songs and prayers; the evil residues of illness must, nevertheless, be exorcised, in Evilway or Weaponway fashion, with the appropriate rites. Each species of Holy People, such as Bear,

---

[1]Evidence of an Evilway version of Coyoteway is presented below, Chapters 11 and 12, with the myth and the sandpaintings of William Charlie. See also an explanation of Evilway modes of performance later in this chapter.

Snake, Wind, or Lightning, requires its own special reconciliation procedures. So it may be said, that each of the twenty or more chant-ways represents a sort of "mini-religion." Each of these small-scale religious traditions has its own distinct soteriology; it saves the devotee, that is, the patient, from his particular predicament and estrangement, yes, even from his self-destructive open rebellion against a divine being. The process of liberation and recovery requires usually a two, five, or nine-night performance of the god's (or gods') own prescribed reconciliation ceremonial.

Adjusted to Pueblo Indian cosmography, the divine Coyote People live underground. At the same time, manifestations of these divine prototypes roam in the surface world as animals. Ma'ii is the Navajo name for Coyote; it is also a generic name for the larger wolf and the smaller foxes. The remaining predators, even snakes, are sometimes included in the extended mạ'ii family.[2] The Coyoteway which is presented here does not include any references to wolves, but according to our informants it includes all the Coyote People who now live in the Navajo territory: White Coyote in the east, Blue Coyote in the south, Yellow Coyote in the west, and Black Coyote in the north. Of these the Yellow Coyote (yellow or red fox) and the Blue Coyote (gray or silver fox) are native in the Black Mesa area. Black Coyote is said to live "somewhere on the Navajo Reservation; he is used in the yé'iibicheii (Nightway) ceremonial" (Luke Cook). Specifically, it is the Gray or Blue Coyote from the south who figures in the last sand-painting ceremony where a yé'ii-impersonator carries a stuffed specimen of the mạ'ii species. In the sandpainting itself, animal-shaped and anthropomorphic Coyote People of all four colors are represented.

For diagnostic purposes the Navajo Coyoteway can be performed as a two-night ceremonial. If it proves effective, a continuation of up to at least five nights is called for, namely, the first four nights (evenings and mornings) of the complete nine-night sequence and a basket-drum summary on the fifth night. The second four-night portion of the full sequence can be considered as a separate ceremony. For historical interpretation, someday, it will be significant to know that the Holiness Rite of the Jicarilla Apache corresponds to the second half of Navajo nine-night ceremonials. The first portion of the Navajo sequence is omitted in the Jicarilla ceremonials (cf. Opler 1943, pp. 94f). Nevertheless, on account of this I do not regard the first four nights of Coyoteway as constituting a later development. On the contrary, the rites on the first four evenings and mornings strike me as

---

[2] Mạ'i is an old Apachean form for "animal." See, for instance, the Chiricahua mbai—coyote; mbai'tso—wolf; mba'ishội—lizard. (Personal communication of Morris E. Opler.)

being, in the Navajo historical context, much more archaic than the Puebloized sandpainting rites which follow. A combination of at least two basically different ceremonial traditions seems, therefore, indicated. In the case of the Navajo Coyoteway the synthesis of two such traditions is indeed firm. While the four-night portions of the ceremonial are separable, patients become eligible for the second portion only after having experienced the first portion earlier.

In contrast to Luke Cook, whose Coyote theology of cosmic dimensions has already been introduced, our Coyoteway singer, Man With Palomino Horse, insists on a simpler explanation—that Coyote illness results only from offending animal Coyote persons. According to him, prior to 1948, or thereabouts, a bounty was paid on the Navajo Reservation for coyote skins. Apparently this was a government effort at reducing the ever-increasing livestock losses, especially among young lambs. But this well-intentioned measure burdened the coyote-hunting shepherds with divinely caused troubles and with human guilt. Not many centuries ago the Navajo people were hunters. Coyote was a fellow hunter who probably enjoyed the rights of kinship which then applied to all fellow hunter peoples. As the explanations to some of William Charlie's sandpaintings (Chapter 12) seem to indicate, Coyote functioned occasionally, though definitely more seldom than his big brother Wolf, as a divine tutelary power in hunting.

Still in the 1880s Coyote was regarded as a respectable hunter tutelary among the Zuni Indians. Frank H. Cushing (1920, pp. 414-515) has recorded a mythological narrative about a hunter whose divine sponsor and guardian was a Coyote person. It seems at least possible that the portion of the Zuni story, which refers directly to the Hunter/Coyote relationship, has had parallels in other hunter traditions of the Southwest. Numerous incidents from Navajo coyote mythology can be traced to Pueblo Indian traditions. Moreover, William Charlie's Navajo Coyoteway could be performed for success in hunting.

In any case, later, when the Navajo hunters had become herdsmen provisioned with and equipped by Western materialism, they were hunting coyotes as nuisances and pests. This all too sudden change to a pursuit of new values took its toll. Coyote illness soon was on the increase and was persistently diagnosed in the Black Mesa area. Since 1948, according to our practitioner, Coyote troubles have been declining steadily in this area.

The manner in which Coyote illness is caught was explained by our singer in the following manner: When a Coyote person is shot and left to die, his last spasms and twitchings, as they suddenly cease in the animal person, leap onto the killer. This happens most easily if somehow in the process of killing the hunter has eye-contact with his victim—Coyote continues to recognize and to haunt the offender. But this can also happen through physical contact with the animal's dead body or even with the decayed remains of a Coyote person. And in this regard no shepherd who strolls through the sagebrush pastures can ever be sure of his personal immunity. Killing a Coyote person means offending him. The symptoms of the animal's suffering which are thrown onto the offender continue as a sort of nervous malfunction, as a shaking of the head, hands, or of the entire body.

Coyote illness may also be indicated by a twisted mouth, by cross-eyed vision, by weakened eyesight, loss of memory or loss of mind, and by fainting (Luke Cook). Earlier sources (Franciscan Fathers 1910, p. 363) counted mania and prostitution (sex frenzy) among the symptoms of Coyote illness. Wyman and Kluckhohn (1938, p. 27, informant "R") named prostitution, mania and rabies. Their informant "M" added sore throat and stomach trouble. Recently I have even been told of a case where chronic alcoholism was diagnosed as Coyote illness. Notwithstanding possible later embellishments, mania, nervous malfunctions, and rabies seem to comprise the basic symptom pattern of Coyote illness most naturally. What our practitioner has described as shaking and twitching may well be traceable to rabies. This seems even more likely if we consider that our patient, after he is initiated into a sort of kinship with Coyote peoples, must also respect dogs, wild cats, badgers, porcupines, and skunks—all potential carriers of rabies.

Nevertheless, these considerations do not allow us to simply reduce the Coyoteway healing procedure to a primitive attempt to cure rabies. No scientific experiment has yet disproven the link between rabies and the intentions of some divine Coyote peoples—not to mention the intentions of the cosmic Coyote who transmits his spells on humankind from beyond Sun and Moon in the east. First and foremost in the perspective of the Coyoteway tradition is the wrath of divine Coyote people, and it must be placated.

Meanwhile, for the majority of the Navajo people Coyote has lost his positive value and function. Some people on the reservation barely seem to know anymore that the shakedowns (the dust or "pollen" brushed from a coyote being) contain power to procure wealth. Most people have by now come to interpret the sighting of a coyote as a bad omen. Like many things which still had their proper place in the old Navajo hunter tradition, and like his big brother Wolf, Coyote has come to be associated with witchcraft.

This defamation of Coyote as a divine person appears to be the result of two parallel developments. The first is that all hunter gods eventually suffer defamation if their human protégés cease to be hunters and if they learn to answer to different types of gods (cf. Luckert 1975, pp. 186-90). Coyote is a trickster person *par excellence*. Among archaic hunters this reputation gave him prestige; hunters daily tried to imitate his trickery.[3] But trickster gods among presiding shepherds or among sedentary planters are a nuisance—their archaic behavior burdens them soon with the reputation of being wizards or even of being devils. In spite of all this, Coyote does nothing to redeem his reputation—he kills the shepherds' lambs. According to what seems to belong to the Pueblo Indian portion of Coyote mythology, this trickster also steals the farmers' maize.

There is a second reason for Coyote's bad reputation. Aside from suffering the universal fate of all hunter gods in post-hunting cultures, Coyote, while getting involved in medicinal ceremonialism, came under suspicion precisely from that direction. Luke Cook, our patient, traces every kind of illness to the great Coyote beyond Sun and Moon in the east; and as far as Coyote's general disposition can be understood—"Coyote giveth and Coyote taketh away." So it seems that the present defamation of Coyote is being generated also by that same general concern which necessitates various versions of Evilway healing ceremonials.[4] Evilway performances emphasize exorcism and are held primarily to drive away vengeful ghosts, their bewitching influence, together with evil hosts of other witchcraft elements. Evilway ceremonials today run a close second in popularity to the Blessingway rites. Their popularity, it seems, runs parallel with the general fear of ghost-influence in Navajo society. Fears of various kinds marry each other easily.[5] In any case, it must be noted, that the *deezláji* (Weapon- or

---

[3]Apache tribes used Coyote ceremonies for trickery of war (personal communication of Morris E. Opler). On the other hand, it was insisted on by the participants, that sexual trickery, which is frequently attributed to Coyote, has nothing to do with the performance of the Coyoteway ceremonial which is recorded in this book.

[4]Evilway rites became increasingly necessary during the Fort Sumner period (see Chapter 2). Also in Chapter 2, note 2, Coyote's involvement in Pueblo Indian witchcraft is documented.

[5]I have delineated my incomplete views on this subject in *The Navajo Hunter Tradition* (pp. 199-202). The increase in the fear of ghost-influence, in Navajo history, appears to have been primarily the result of having lost touch with the traditional "Black Earth" eschatology. According to an informant of Wyman, Hill, and Osanai (1942, pp. 34-37), the dead Navajo people formerly went to join their predecessors who had returned to Black Earth, a northern place. It seems that upon moving south, in confrontation with Pueblo Indian emergence mythology, and with an evergrowing dedication of practitioners to retain their patients' health at any cost, apparitions of the dead ceased to be tolerable signals for rejoining the ancestors. For people who refuse to be escorted away—at least "not yet"—ghost apparitions are bad omens. For people who no longer know where to go after death they are evil in general and a threat to human existence.

Morris E. Opler (personal communication) suggested that defeat, loss of territory in the face of a growing population, lack of resources, high incidence of disease, alcoholism, etc., cause friction and suspicion among Navajos; further, that these human conflicts, the ill will and suspicions which they engender, play a large part in the perpetuation of the fear of ghosts and witches. This statement does indeed explain the intensification of fears in certain culture areas. But it also appears that religious eschatologies do not necessarily obey the laws of economics, anatomy, or psychology. The same troubles which in one place intensify interpersonal conflicts and subsequent fears, are resolved elsewhere by the

Fightingway) attitude which is expressed in Evilway rites against certain causes of disease—whether they be ghosts, witches, or defamed archaic gods—is the opposite of the search for reconciliation which predominates during Holyway rites. And having been caught in this general trend of Evilway thinking, Coyote has become associated with the "wrong kind of people."

In several versions of Evilway mythology—as in Upwardreaching-way and in the myth of Ghostway in the Male Branch of Shooting-way—Coyote is no longer mentioned in Holyway fashion as an offended deity, a subsequent patient, or as a reconciling agent of health; instead, he is regarded exclusively as a cause of illness. In this manner Coyote has become identified with vengeful ghosts and with evil witchcraft elements with whom reconciliation is no longer possible. Coyote, the already defamed hunter tutelary roaming among shepherds, must now be driven away—exorcised in order to safeguard human health. And so it seems that, because of an increase in Evilway-type thinking, this Holyway-type ceremonial was increasingly mis-understood and avoided. Had it not been for the government's bounty on coyote skins, which produced a flare-up of Coyote illness and a demand for the ceremonial in the conservative Black Mesa area, the Coyoteway ceremonial of the Holyway type would probably not have survived. But now, after several decades of inroads made by American secular education, it seems as though this religious ceremonial is definitely doomed.

While his ceremonial is disappearing, Coyote as an archaic divine figure is still a long way from dying. Indeed, he was forced into joining the ranks of antiquated and defamed hunter gods, but Coyote myth-ology itself credits him with several resurrections. His positive role is still vaguely reflected in the ethicized fables which depict the great Coyote of Coyoteway as a laughable villain, buffoon, or bungler—more often than as a shrewd exemplary model for hunter tricksters. The archaic Coyote, the epitome of hunter tricksters, could indeed be a clownish bungler. Divine incarnations among hunters need this sign of humanity. On the other hand, the Coyote of Coyoteway is also a greater-than-human personage, a deity who, when angered, inflicts his brand of punishment or illness and who, when reconciled with the use of his own prayers, songs, and rites, restores the patient to health. He even helps a man to gain prosperity.

---

vision of a real afterworld in favor of a harmonious coexistence with the dead. Proof of this has been the Ghost Dance religion toward the end of the nineteenth century on the Great Plains. And, while fear of witches appears to linger today in the Navajo Peyote religion, frequent anticipation of "a new heaven and a new earth" has generally transformed fear of the dead into a realationship of friendship with them.

The strongly ethicized, popular Coyote tales which until now have been available in ethnological literature represent, as all ethical systems do, only the tail end or afterglow of a religious fascination. The real Coyoteway ceremonial was classified as "extinct" by the Franciscan Fathers in 1910 (p. 392). From the perspective of a historian of religions it seems therefore extremely fortunate that the archaic core of Coyote religion among the Navajo, the "head of the comet," so to speak, could once more be sighted and seen in a meaningful historical context.

*   *   *

A brief explanation about nomenclature may be in order at this point. A Navajo healing ceremonial is called a *hatáál*, a "sing." The person who officiates is a *hataałi*, a "singer." However, almost everywhere in the Western world the word "singer" conjures up some associations with operas and folk music. In my earlier work on the Navajo hunter tradition I have used, with some hesitation, the popular term "medicine man." Leland Wyman has advised strongly against using this term in connection with Coyoteway. "Medicine man" reminds him of America's once popular medicine shows. Obviously, Navajo healing ceremonies should not be confused with unscrupulous salesmanship and with a circus atmosphere. Wyman, who is also a scholar of biology and physiology, suggests that the term "practitioner" be used.

As far as the title "shaman" is concerned, I am still very sympathetic toward Mircea Eliade's delineation of shamanism as "techniques of ecstasy." At the same time, I see that outside the Tungusic-Siberian realm shamanism is not always clearly definable in terms of ecstasy. In the American Indian area a rational discourse with the god(s) often takes the place of ecstasy. Moreover, individuals who would be better classified as priests sometimes have ecstatic experiences. Morris Opler suggests therefore that Navajo ceremonialists be distinguished from shamans by virtue of their reliance on traditions. Thus, a shaman who no longer alters his rite on the basis of direct communication with divine tutelaries and on the spur of the moment, should be called a priest. This line of demarcation extends the phenomenon of shamanism just enough to accomodate the American Indian situation. Since ecstasy is a matter of degrees and is an inner happening, detection is often very difficult. For field research in American Indian religions the boundary line which is suggested by Opler is therefore more useful. Moreover, since the Tungusic terminus "shaman" has already been linked to loosely related phenomena elsewhere in the world, this slight adaptation seems justified.

Theologically defined, this means then that a shaman should be regarded as having become a priestly practitioner when his divine tutelary (or tutelaries) no longer adds new revelations to his rite. Therefore, wherever in this book I mention Navajo "shamanism" or refer to "shamans" I actually have reference to a time when the northern religious heritage of Apachean hunters was still intact— a time, perhaps, before the Spanish name "Navajo" was applied.

Our Coyoteway ceremonialist may thus be called a practitioner, or else, he may be called a priest. I like the term "practitioner" because it implies a professional relationship toward individual clients; I dislike the term because in our Western culture it generally refers to a materialistically trained, scientific medical doctor. I like the designation "priest" because it refers to a mediator between god(s) and humankind; I dislike the term because priests are generally thought of as mediating between god(s) and organized groups of people. Navajo singers perform their ceremonials for individual clients. In an attempt to get the best part of both suggestions I have decided, in this book, to refer to our ceremonialist primarily as "priestly practitioner." In order to escape the awkward grammatical consequences of this long title, I will occasionally substitute such alternatives as healer, practitioner, priest, singer, and priestly singer.

The primary participants in the Coyoteway ceremonial, the divine Coyote People and various other divine personages, I prefer to call "gods." In much of anthropological literature the term "supernatural(s)" has been adopted. In my opinion this is a most unfortunate choice. To apply this term in Navajo religion, where nature is not yet distinguished from a divine realm, would be more distortive than simply referring to gods as greater-than-human personal powers or Holy People.

*   *   *

Finally, an explanation is called for concerning the capitalization of some English nouns in translations of Navajo texts. The practice of writing ordinary English nouns with small letters, and of capitalizing the names of persons, is based on a view of the world where the observers pretend to know, absolutely, the difference between an "object" and a "person." This practice is a legacy of British Empiricism and the result of scientific ambitions. But, unlike English orthography, Navajo traditional thought has none of its roots in this philosophy. Navajo traditionalists are obviously capable of identifying certain less-than-human entities as "objects" or as "things," but, when on subsequent occasions some of these "objects" happen to reveal themselves as persons, then traditionally oriented Navajo minds remain open also to this possibility. When in addition such entities that are recognized as persons are seen as being in some ways greater-than-human, they are approached as Holy People, accordingly, with prayers and with songs. The least an editor can do in rendering these prayers and songs, and in describing the Navajo religious posture in English, is to refer to what may be Holy People by way of capitalized "proper" nouns.

Man With Palomino Horse
and His Tradition

The Singer and His Teachers

He lives in one of the southern valleys of Black Mesa, approximately five miles from Piñon. A big man, he stands broader and taller than most of his fellow tribesmen, even now that he is well advanced in years. Various estimates of his age, as being somewhere in the eighties, were given by people who know him. At the time of the ceremonial he himself answered that he was now seventy-seven years old.

We do not know how soon among his tribesmen our practitioner became known as Man With Palomino Horse. Presumably he had to be old enough to own an easily distinguishable horse with a white mane. In those days, we can infer, the man's horse was more conspicuous than its rider. The people named the rider after his horse. The horse has long since died, the singer has become an important person in his own right, but he is still known as the man of that famous palomino horse. Our singer, who today is known among his fellow tribesmen as an accomplished practitioner of Coyoteway and of Lifeway (Female Shooting Branch), and as one who assists in the performance of various other song ceremonials, must be searched for in the United States census books under a different name. Man With Palomino Horse— *hastiin bitsiigha' łigaii hólónii,* of the Coyote Clan—seemed an impossible designation to the government official who was given the difficult task of recording the man's existence. With an unusual flare of imagination this unknown official assigned him a name not much shorter than the original name would have been: Jessie James Begay the First.

Man With Palomino Horse said he learned the Coyoteway ceremonial from Many Whiskers *(bidághaa' łáni)* who died in the middle fifties. His former apprentice, Luke Cook, mentioned the maternal uncle of Man With Palomino Horse, Yellow Hair *(tsii' łitsooí)*, as an intermediary teacher. So it appears that Yellow Hair was an older apprentice of Many Whiskers while Man With Palomino Horse was a younger one. When Many Whiskers died, the Man With Palomino Horse finished learning Coyoteway by observing Yellow Hair. Many Whiskers, the grandfather who taught Yellow Hair and Man With Palomino Horse, learned the Coyoteway ceremonial from another and older grandfather, He Who Returns Angrily *(hashkéé náane)*, who died when our practitioner was only six years old—thus around 1903.

When given the name *hastiin neez* to identify, the face of Man With Palomino Horse lit up. Yes, he knew *hastiin neez*. From him he has the sandpaintings which were used in our ceremonial. This piece of information needs some slight modification, perhaps. Mary Wheelwright wrote that *hastiin neez*, from near Rainbow Bridge, died in 1919. At that time Man With Palomino Horse was only twenty-two years old. It is quite possible that he saw *hastiin neez* use the sandpaintings in question. But it should also be taken into account that in 1929, Many Whiskers gave to Laura Armer exactly the same sandpaintings. Many Whiskers was a direct teacher of Man With Palomino Horse until the fifties; so it would seem natural that our practitioner's knowledge about the sandpaintings of *hastiin neez* was reinforced through him.

Both grandfathers, He Who Returns Angrily and Many Whiskers, were included when in 1864 Navajo people were deported to the Fort Sumner concentration camp. According to his age, it is possible that *hastiin neez*, who died in 1919, was included also. This episode of existential fears and hostilities—when the Navajos were surrounded by the United States Army, felt threatened by "Enemy Navajos," Mescaleros, Comanches, and Kiowas, and when their number was reduced by famine and epidemics—has visibly increased the Navajo awareness of witchcraft. At that time Evilway rites were primarily called for. Father Berard (1950, p. 297) reported that at that time a Chiricahua Apache introduced a sucking cure, which was aimed specifically against the disease producing agents of "bean-shooting" witchcraft. This intensified confrontation could well have contributed some aspects to the present form of the Coyoteway ceremonial. Perhaps "Burning the Feathers," the counter-measure for "feather-shooting," was added then (cf. note 2, this chapter).

Man With
Palomino Horse,
Coyoteway singer.

Hastiin Neez.

This photograph
—from the Philip
Johnston Collection,
Special Collections,
Northern Arizona
University Library—
was identified by
Man With
Palomino Horse
as his teacher of
long ago.

Man with Palomino Horse seemed unable to name a still older Coyoteway singer. However, Luke Cook, who belongs to the last generation of Coyoteway apprentices, has heard it spoken that the first Coyoteway singer who taught the above mentioned grandfathers was Yellow Man of the Canyon People *(tséyi' niiłtsooi)*. Presumably this man had already died when the Navajo people were taken to Fort Sumner. All agree, nevertheless, that Coyoteway was known and had been performed in Navajoland long before the Fort Sumner deportation.

Where historical inquiries end, the mythical record usually points a little farther. Both Coyoteway myths of the Holyway type (given in Chapters 9 and 10) point to a place of origin in the La Plata Mountains, in the Mesa Verde vicinity. Whether Luke Cook's "Yellow Man of the Canyon People" is identical with the "Nalth-keh-olth-eh" of *tséyi'nii* or with the "Grandnephew of the Coyote-clan chief" of *yoo' hataałii* (see Chapters 10, 11), is now impossible to verify. In any case, what the two myths agree on is that the Coyoteway ceremonial originated in the Old Navajoland—the place where according to its cosmological orientation one would expect it to have originated. Old Navajoland is the place where Navajo-Apachean hunter shamans first seem to have come in contact with the Pueblo Indian four-directional four-level cosmology and with the anthropogony of emergence. Courageous shamans that they were, a few of them ventured down into the hole of emergence from where, according to the new world view, all life and power originates. Coyote and fox tutelaries have been showing their fellow hunters the right way all along—by digging burrows for themselves and by living in the "underworld." Now, at last, in the light of the Pueblo myth of emergence, could the pioneering efforts and hints of the Coyote People be fully understood.

The Mythico-historical Origin of Coyoteway

When Man With Palomino Horse told the story about the origin of Coyoteway he emphasized that this is the only story that belonged to the ceremonial from the beginning. He admitted that some storytellers may have added additional Coyote stories, but this story is all that belongs.

Rock-extending-between (Middle Point) is the name of the place. It snowed early in the morning. A man was going out with the intention to hunt. He saw Coyote tracks. He started backtracking the Coyote tracks. They led to a pond which was surrounded with many

kinds of green plants. As he approached he saw a ladder sticking out of
the water, barely above the water. On the steps of this ladder the
hunter went down into the water.[1] Down below he touched ground.
It was very beautiful down there. The earth surface on which we now
sit had winter; there was snow on the ground. But below it was
summer; there was green grass, flowers, all over the place. In the east
he saw white buildings. He went over to the buildings and saw Coyote
human beings. They were in fact human beings, but they were Coyote
People. There were lots of young beautiful girls with long and wavy
hair. Then he saw all the fields of corn. The corn was ripe. The Coyote
People gathered the corn and cooked meals for him. He ate and stayed
overnight.

Toward evening the Coyote People assembled, and he was taught
the Coyoteway ceremonial—the songs, the prayers, the procedures,
and the prayersticks. He was taught everything. He simply learned it
from these people. They told him that the prayers, the songs, and the
ceremonial items are also to be used on the earth; and these are the
ways you are going to use them. These were all read to him. It seems,
perhaps, that he wrote it all on papers of his mind. Then he began
climbing up again to this earth. He came up through the water, on the
ladder, to the earth.

So this is the simple story about where the songs and the ceremonial came from. So this is what it is. This is what my grandfather
told me; Many Whiskers is his name. Further back in time there was
another grandfather who died of old age, his name is He Who Returns
Angrily. He died when I was only six years old. The other grandfather
died more recently, about twenty years ago. So these are the people
from whom I have learned it. They taught me these things, and I
accepted them. I learned them. And that is the way it is today. It is
a simple story. And this is all.

---

[1]The setting of this myth, with "a ladder sticking out of the water," is identical in all the three
available Coyoteway versions of the Holyway type. The two other versions by *yoo' hataałii* and by
tséyi'nii, are given in Chapters 9-10. A related Lipan Apache story can be found in Morris E. Opler's
Myths and Legends of the Lipan Apache Indians, 1940, pp. 41-44. The setting in all these myths is
obviously related to Pueblo *kiva* architecture and to the mythic flood caused by the Water Serpent (see
Luckert 1976). The origin myth of the Hopi Reed clan appears to have provided the model for Coyoteway
cosmology. The myth of the Hopi Snake clan, in some of its aspects, may be the prototype for the Reed
clan myth. What is unique in the ecstatic journey of the Navajo shaman can be seen after subtracting the
Hopi elements from the available Coyoteway myths.

The Hopi Reed clan hero went in search of a hunting animal. From the crest of a mountain he
sighted a dog. The animal trotted ahead of him and led him "to what appeared to be a water hole.
Protruding from the water was the top of a ladder. The dog began to descend the ladder, and as he did so
the water disappeared." Spider Grandmother advised the man to follow: "...this is the *kiva* of the dog
people." The hero obtained a hunting dog to take home with him. In the origin myth of the Snake clan the
ancestral hero married a Snake maiden and learned how to perform the Snake ceremonies (Courlander
1971, pp. 58, 103-5). Thus it appears that the Navajo Coyoteway myth of the Holyway type is a blend of
Hopi Reed clan cosmology, of something akin to Hopi Snake clan initiational procedures, and of Navajo
shamanic experience and/or ingenuity.

On two occasions we asked Luke Cook about what he knows concerning the origin of the Coyoteway ceremonial. In the first instance he referred simply to the mythic age immediately after the emergence of the first people from the underworld. Everything else in human history began with First Man, First Woman, First Boy, First Girl, and Coyote, so why should the Coyoteway ceremonial not be traceable to these? On the second occasion, while explaining the Feather-burning Rite, he told us the myth of Coyote's adventure into Narrow Canyon. When later we asked Man With Palomino Horse specifically about this myth, he claimed that, while it explains the Feather-burning Rite, it has nothing to do with Coyoteway; moreover, it belongs to the Upwardreaching Chant *(hanełnéhe)* which serves the primary purpose of driving away the evil influence of ghosts, witches, and Coyote. Concerning a first Coyoteway ceremonial on the rim of Narrow Canyon, about which Luke Cook informed us, our practitioner seemed to know nothing. Nevertheless, Luke Cook's story is verified by earlier recordings; it contains important historical data, coming from a time when the idea of feather-burning was introduced and when Evilway-type thinking not only pressured but also shaped the apologetics of the Holyway-type Coyoteway. There was, in fact, a Coyoteway ceremonial performed on the rim of Narrow Canyon. The mischievous Coyote was indeed chased out of Narrow Canyon, but not, as Evilway singers maintain, because he was Evil incarnate. Rather, Coyote became a patient—thus the prototype of all subsequent patients and healers. Divine Coyote People came to heal their kinsman. Thus, Coyote is not the evil being which, according to Evilway mythology, only deserves to be driven away. Coyote is a person; more yet, Coyote is a Navajo.

The Coyoteway originated at Narrow Canyon *(tséyi' haats'ósí)*. The Bird People lived in this canyon under ledges along the cliffs. Coyote ventured among them and angered them. In revenge the Bird People shot their feathers into Coyote. They were using these feathers as witchcraft arrows—shooting them like feathered arrows. Coyote barely escaped to the top of the canyon. He felt miserable.[2]

[2]According to a Taos tale (Parsons 1940, pp. 112-15), Coyote became envious of clothing which White-headed Eagles possessed. They agreed to trade some of their clothing if Coyote would get for them a blue coyote fur. To accomplish his end Coyote plays dead while all kinds of coyotes examine his condition—Red Coyote, Gray Coyote, Black Coyote, and Blue Coyote. In the process Coyote kills Blue Coyote, skins him, and trades the fur for the Eagles' clothes....

Up to this point—if we assume Navajo borrowing from Pueblo mythology—this story explains

Luke Cook on horseback, with Mrs. Cook and son,
on the day of the author's first visit to his homestead, in 1971.

The Reverend Johnny C. Cooke,
friend, interpreter and resourceful guide.

Then Coyote came to the home of Horned Toad and there he asked for food. He demanded to be given all the available food. Horned Toad refused. Thereupon Coyote became angry and swallowed him. He thought he had killed him. And Coyote sat in Horned Toad's house, his hogan. Shshd! Coyote heard a sound and concluded that he was in a *ch'įįdii hooghan*; he was feeling increasingly worse. (The humorous implication is what every child knows: if Coyote had actually killed Horned Toad and had dispatched his ghost, the hogan would indeed be *hok'ee*—a ghost hogan. The ghost of Horned Toad would naturally claim the home in which he was dispatched.)

Meanwhile, Horned Toad who was still alive crawled all around in Coyote's belly, exploring it. He wondered what all the different organs were and grabbed them as he investigated—stomach, lungs, and the heart. At last he pinched off the heart and came out through the mouth. There was blood in the mouth and face of Coyote, stemming from his internal bleeding. For the time being Horned Toad had killed Coyote.[3]

At this point the narrator broke off, but from subsequent conversations it became obvious that because of his self-provoked sufferings, because of his "coyoteing around," Coyote has himself become the first Coyoteway patient. This happened up on the rim of Narrow Canyon where other Coyote People had gathered to revive him. This conclusion of the myth transforms a potential Evilway myth into one of the Holyway type. Coyote does not remain the epitome of Evil; rather, he becomes the prototype of all subsequent Coyoteway patients and healers. According to the ancient way of Coyote all subsequent sufferers—though they may have brought their suffering upon themselves through "coyoteing around"—are given a chance for recovery. Divine grace and participation abounds over merit.

---

perhaps the curious fact of why in Coyoteway coyotes are constantly mentioned and why the skin of a "blue coyote" (gray fox) and a stuffed "blue coyote" are actually used.

The Taos tale continues: ...Encouraged by his improved appearance, Coyote challenges the Eagles to a fight; this time his personal clothing, his own skin, is to be at stake. In the course of the fight the powerful Eagles shoot "very little, fine arrows" into Coyote. Coyote is defeated and loses his skin.

This "feather-shooting" episode seems to extend the Pueblo mythological influence to the Navajo Evilway Upwardreaching ceremonial—eventually even to the present Evilway intrusion of Coyoteway itself. Coyote's association with witchcraft seems otherwise well documented in the Pueblo realm. Parsons informs us that "most Pueblo witch transformations are into Coyote" and that frequently in mythology Coyote is also regarded as the First Witch (Parsons 1939, pp. 217, 1067n). In addition, a "Feather-burning Rite" has been reported from Zuni (Ladd 1960, p. 118).

[3] A related myth is given in the narrative by *tséyi'nii* (Chapter 10, paragraphs 21-28.). See also the introductory statement to this myth.

PART TWO:

COYOTEWAY
PERFORMED

The Nine-Night Sequence

The nine-night Coyoteway ceremonial divides naturally into two four-night portions and a one-night summary. Each of the four-night portions is further divisible into an evening and a morning section. This enables us to discuss the ceremonial as five groups of ceremonies: Unraveling Ceremonies, Fire Ceremonies, Basket-Drum Ceremonies, Sandpainting Ceremonies, and the Ninth-Night Summary.

During the nine-night sequence of the Coyoteway ceremonial many songs are chanted. All have been recorded on tape and are presented here in the form of a free English translation. Johnny Cooke usually dictated to me from the tapes, sentence by sentence, what he considered to be the best English translation. Sentence by sentence, in return, I suggested alternate formulations by utilizing the largest possible number of synonyms. In addition, Johnny Cooke frequently explained different contexts in which certain Navajo expressions are used. Whenever we were in doubt about a particular word or phrase, we took it to Luke Cook or to Man With Palomino Horse to have it explained. In the end, the task of editing and balancing the lines fell on me. While it would be foolish to insist that every word in these songs is translated with unambiguous precision, both Johnny Cooke and I are satisfied that we have done what honestly could be done with this difficult archaic material. For the specialist there will always be copies of tapes which we deposited at the Navajo Tribal Museum, Window Rock, at the Museum of Navaho Ceremonial Art, Santa Fe, at the Museum of Northern Arizona, Flagstaff, and at the Smithsonian Institution.

For presenting the entire ceremonial as an illustrated documentary, it has seemed best to group the various ceremonies together with their repetitions from subsequent days. So, for instance, the Unraveling Ceremonies of the first four evenings are discussed as one unit, regardless of there having been Fire Ceremonies on the mornings between. Combining repetitions into a single discussion makes for easier reading and comprehension; however, it interrupts the actual recording sequence. In order to remedy this difficulty and to facilitate easy checking on the actual song and prayer sequence, a continuously numbered index is here provided. Numbers in parentheses indicate earlier occasions in the sequence where the same song has been chanted.

The Nine-Night Sequence of Coyoteway

EVENING AND NIGHT	MORNING AND NOON
1. Unraveling Ceremony	
	Fire Ceremony
2. Unraveling Ceremony	
	Fire Ceremony
3. Unraveling Ceremony	
	Fire Ceremony
4. Unraveling Ceremony	
	Fire Ceremony
5. Basket-drum Ceremony	
	Sandpainting Ceremony, One-*yé'ii*
6. Basket-drum Ceremony	
	Sandpainting Ceremony, One-*yé'ii*
7. Basket-drum Ceremony	
	Sandpainting Ceremony, One-*yé'ii*
8. Basket-drum Ceremony	
	Sandpainting Ceremony, Three-*yé'ii*
9. Basket-drum Summary	

Index to Song and Prayer Sequence of Coyoteway

First Evening

1. They were given
2. Now it has begun moving
3. With these he is well again
4. By these he was led
5. Hwii eiya eiya! The sound was heard

First Morning

6. By sternness, whatever your name is
7. I bring these to you
8. Formal Prayer
9. He has walked
10. This is the Fur
11. The Red Berry Shrubs
12. It is his Water
13. He who was given
14. The Red Berry Shrubs (cont.)
15. The Furs are put in the water

Second Evening

16. The stick stands upright
17. With these he is well again (3)
18. With these he walked
19. With these he ran
20. By these he was led (4)
21. The sound was heard (5)

Second Morning

22. I bring these to you (7)
23. Formal Prayer
24. He has walked (9)
25. This is the Hogan
26. On these he walked
27. The Medicine is being made
28. The Medicine is ready
29. The Medicine I ate
30. The furs are put in the water (15)

Third Evening

31. He brought it back
32. Now it has begun moving (2)
33. With these he is well again (3, 17)
34. With these he walked (18)
35. By these he was led (4, 20)
36. The sound was heard (5, 21)

Index to Song and Prayer Sequence of Coyoteway (cont.)

Index to Song and Prayer Sequence of Coyoteway (cont.)

Seventh Morning

101. From the Hogans I came down (86, 95)
102. From the hidden Hogan I came with herbs (87, 96)
103. Beneath the Two Rising, he ran (88, 97)

Eighth Evening

104. With my Mind I walk
105. I am looking for my mind
106. I have found my Mind
107. I am bringing back my Mind
108. I am reviving my Mind
109. Now my Mind is walking with me
110. Now my Mind is remade for me
111. Now my Mind returns with me
112. Now I am sitting with my Mind
113. With Black Bead as my feet, with this I walk
114. They are singing for me
115. It is raining on me
116. The blessing is given

Eighth Morning

117. Hwii eiya eiya, he calls me
118. White Bead Son is touching him
119. The White Bead Son I am
120. Beneath the Two Rising he is moving
121. All is Happiness, all is well
122. From the Hogans I came down (86, 95, 101)
123. From the hidden Hogan I came with herbs (87, 96, 102)
124. Beneath the Two Rising, he ran (88, 97, 103)

Ninth Night

125 through 161.
All songs of fifth, sixth, seventh, and eighth evenings are repeated.

Unraveling Ceremonies

PREPARATIONS AND SINGING

The Unraveling Ceremony is performed on each of the first four evenings of the nine-night Coyoteway ceremonial. The action pattern on each of these performances is rather consistent—except for the number of *wooltáád* bundles that are used and for a variation among songs. Thus, for the purpose of illustrating the procedures, all four evenings can be discussed together.

In preparation for the Unraveling Ceremony on the first evening five *wooltáád* bundles are made. For the second evening of unraveling seven bundles are needed. Nine *wooltáád* bundles are prepared for the third evening. Eleven bundles are required in the fourth Unraveling Ceremony.

Each *wooltáád* bundle contains an eagle feather *(atsá bit'a')*, blue grama grass *(tł'oh nastasi)*, snakeweed *(ch'il diilyésii)*, Artemisia frigida *(tóyikááł)*, rock sagebrush *(tsé'ézhiih)*, and a spruce twig *(ch'ó)*. The bundles are wound and tied with strings spun of sheep wool. At the end of these strings additional eagle feathers are secured to serve as handles during the unraveling. The patient undresses during the last stages of bundle-making.

In a seashell the practitioner mixes *zaa'nił* powder with water: "medicine to be put in the mouth." *Zaa'nił* is ground-up medicine powder made of blue, yellow, and white corn, ground together with fruits from sumac berry *(tsiiłchin)*, juniper *(gad)*, service berry *(dzídzé dit'ódii)*, ribes *(dík'óozhii)*, and "redberry" *(łichíi'ii)* bushes.

[31]

For the second evening of unraveling seven bundles are needed.

Nine *wooltáád* bundles are prepared for the third evening.

Eleven bundles are required in the fourth Unraveling Ceremony.

The bundles are wound and tied with strings spun of sheep wool.
At the end of these strings additional eagle feathers are secured to serve as
handles during the unraveling.

In a bowl the practitioner prepares *kétłoh*, a mixture of four kinds of crushed leaves, suspended in hot water. *Kétłoh* is "rub-on medicine." The leaves for this mixture are obtained from Brickellia grandiflora, "the herb from the air" *(bił haazhch'ih)*, Pectis angustifolia, "the herb from the rock" *(tsé ghánítch'ih)*, "the herb from the water" *(tó bits'ą́ądę́ę́')* and "the frosted herb" *(shohch'il)*. *Zaa'nił* shell and *kétłoh* bowl are illustrated in connection with the One-*yé'ii* Sandpainting Ceremonies in Chapter 7.

The patient's place in the hogan is prepared by sprinkling a cornmeal circle. This circle represents the world. Lines are sprinkled from the center of the circle to its eastern, western, southern, and its northern limits. The result is a wheel-like pattern with four spokes, with the spokes pointing to the four cardinal points of the world. This inner design does not represent a cross extending over the world—such an idea would be too Christian. Nor is this design merely a symbol of the world in its entirety with its four cardinal directions—this idea would be too Pueblo Indian. As perceived by the Navajo participants in the Coyoteway ceremonial, the "lines leading out represent all the living minds" of the world. The participants in our ceremonial recognize "minds" and "persons" wherein most Western people would not even see animate beings.

The patient, who in accordance with ceremonial practice has disrobed, circles the fire sunwise and then sits on this miniature cornmeal world. While the priestly singer intones a series of chants, the patient joins all the living minds and creatures in the world and so symbolically acknowledges his kinship with them. "The world of living minds will speak from the cornmeal design to me." These are the words by which the patient later explained his participation. "There is a relationship of trust, and one will strive in this context to think good thoughts: I will live a long life and die of ripe old-age. I will walk happily. I will walk well. I will finish my life in old age."

After he sits down, the patient, because he is an initiatory and not an actually suffering patient, joins the practitioner and his helpers in the singing. On the rapturous wings of traditional songs the leader, especially, is transported into another space—the real world where underworld and surface-world have blended into one. With his rattle he maintains an ecstatic rhythm—restructuring the neutral flow of past, present, and future into the eternally returning heartbeats of sacred time. The first song participates in the primeval moment in the Coyoteway tradition when the holy Coyote People, in the underworld, consecrated the agents of health for the benefit of future patients and apprentices.

"The world of living minds will speak from the cornmeal design to me...."

After he sits down, the patient... joins the practitioner and
his helpers in the singing.

Score of First Coyoteway Song

INTRODUCTION

A

éi-yá nei-yee ya-nga ya-nga ya-nga,

B

néi(yá)níláo(áo-áo-áo-áo) éi yee ya,néi(yá)níláo(áo-áo-áo-áo)éi yá ya(ya)(y

C

yee(ya) éí-néi-ní-lá héi, yee(ya) éí-néi-ní-lá héi, nee-ya-nga nee-ya-nga.

FIRST STANZA SUBJECT

```
jó - ho - naa'-éí    (ya) bi - yá- (áo-áo-áo)-ázh
naa - dą́ą́'  ax - gaii (ya) bi - yá- (áo-áo-áo)-ázh
niho- ką́ą́'  k'os dix- hix  biką́ą́'gǫ́ǫ́ (óu-óu-óu- óu)
atsi- niltx'ish bi - ką́ą́'-(aa)- gǫ́ǫ́ (óu-óu-óu- óu)
nixch'-i    dix- hix  (ya) bitx'-ó - (óu-óu-óu)-ól
k'aa' ii' - ni'  (ei  ya) bii - né- íí (é- é- éíí)
```

REFRAIN

--éí yá ya (ya), néi-(ya)-ní-láo (áo-áo-áo-áo) éi yá (ya)(ya),

yee(ya) éí-néi-ní-lá héi, yee(ya) éí-néi-ní-lá héi, nee-ya-nga nee-ya-nga.

BLESSING

są́(ą́)'í naaghą́íí(ą́íí-ą́íí-ą́íí) éí yee ya, bik'eh hózhǫ́(ǫ́-ǫ́-ǫ́-ǫ́) éí yee (ya).

TRANSITION: Tune and articulation as in INTRODUCTION C,B,C.

SECOND STANZA SUBJECT: Tune as in first stanza. REFRAIN

```
tx'éé-hó - naa'-éí    (ya) bi - yá - (áo-áo- áo)-ázh
naa - dą́ą́' axt- sooi (ya) bi - yá - (áo-áo- áo)-ázh
ką́ą́'- áí  dix- hix  (ya) biką́ą́'gǫ́ǫ́ (óu-óu- óu- óu)
nááts'íí - (íí)-lid (ya) xi - gaii-(áo-áo- áo- áo)
nixch'-i   noot-x'i- zhí bi -ts'íis-go (óu-óu- óu)
k'ad éí   na'- nixt'ánii bii - né - íí (é- é- éíí)
```

BLESSING: Tune and articulation as in first stanza.

CONCLUSION: Tune and articulation as in INTRODUCTION C,B,C.

1. Song, First Evening

They were given, they were given,
Those were given, those were given.
The Sons of Sun were given. Those were given, those were given.
The Sons of White Corn were given. Those were given, those were given.
The Dark Cloud above the earth was given. Those were given, those were given.
The Flash of Lightning was given. Those were given, those were given.
The Thin Dark Wind was given. Those were given, those were given.
The Arrow Lightning's Voice was given. Those were given, those were given.
The Long-life One, the Happiness One.
Those were given, those were given,
They were given, they were given,
Those were given, those were given.
The Sons of Moon were given. Those were given, those were given.
The Sons of Yellow Corn were given. Those were given, those were given.
The Ones that stand above were given. Those were given, those were given.
The White Rainbow was given. Those were given, those were given.
The White Wind with its body was given. Those were given, those were given.
The Voice of the Cornripener was given. Those were given, those were given.
The Long-life One, the Happiness One.
Those were given, those were given,
They were given, they were given,
Those were given, those were given.

31. Song, Third Evening, a Continuation of Song 1

He brought it back, he brought it back,
He brought it back, he brought it back.[1]
With these he brought it back.
The Sons of Sun, with these he brought it back.
He brought it back.
The White Corn Boy, with these he brought it back.
He brought it back.

---

[1] Health, Long-life, and Happiness are brought back.

On the rapturous wings of traditional songs the leader, especially,
is transported into another space....

The Black Water, with these he brought it back.
He brought it back.
The White Lightning, with these he brought it back.
He brought it back.
The White Prayerstick, with these he brought it back.
He brought it back.
The Black Prayerstick, with these he brought it back.
He brought it back.
The Black Wind, with these he brought it back.
He brought it back.
The Sound of Thunder, with these he brought it back.
He brought it back.
The Long-life Happiness One, with these he brought it back.
He brought it back, he brought it back,
He brought it back, he brought it back.
With these he brought it back.
The Sons of Moon, with these he brought it back.
He brought it back.
The Sons of Yellow Corn Girl, with these he brought it back.
He brought it back.
The Black Fur, with these he brought it back.
He brought it back.
The White Prayerstick, with these he brought it back.
He brought it back.
The Black Prayerstick, with these he brought it back.
He brought it back.
The White Rainbow, with these he brought it back.
He brought it back.
The Blue Prayerstick, with these he brought it back.
He brought it back.
The Male Cornripener Beetle, with these he brought it back.
He brought it back.
The Long-life Happiness One, with these he brought it back.
He brought it back, he brought it back,
He brought it back, he brought it back.

16, 49. Song, Second and Fourth Evenings

The stick stands upright, the stick stands upright,
The stick stands upright, the stick stands upright.[2]

[2]Reference is made to the vertical stick used in the fire drill. This refrain echoes the fire-making song (Song 6) from the First Morning.

With the Sons of Sun, the stick stands upright.
With the Sons of White Corn, the stick stands upright.
In the White Reed Skin, the stick stands upright.
With Lightning, the stick stands upright.
With Black Wind, the stick stands upright.
With the Sound of Lightning, the stick stands upright.
With the Sons of the Two-who-walk-before-you, Givers of Happiness,
    The stick stands upright, the stick stands upright,
    The stick stands upright, the stick stands upright.
With the Sons of Moon, the stick stands upright.
With the Sons of Yellow Corn Girl, the stick stands upright.
In the Yellow Reed Skin, the stick stands upright.
With the White Rainbow, the stick stands upright.
With Blue Pollen, the stick stands upright.
With the Cornripener, the stick stands upright.
With the Sons of the Two-who-walk-before-you, Givers of Happiness,
    The stick stands upright, the stick stands upright,
    The stick stands upright, the stick stands upright.

2, 32. Song, *First and Third Evenings*

Now it has begun moving, now it has begun moving,
Now it has begun moving, now it has begun moving.
With the help of these it has begun moving.
With the Sons of Sun it has begun moving.
With the Sons of White Corn Girl it has begun moving.
With the Ones that stand above it has begun moving.
With the Flash of Lightning it has begun moving.
With the Black-blossomed Plant, it has begun moving.
With the Sound of Lightning it has begun moving.
With the Long-life Happiness One it has begun moving.
    Now it has begun moving, now it has begun moving,
    Now it has begun moving, now it has begun moving.
With the Sons of Moon it has begun moving.
With the Sons of Yellow Corn it has begun moving.
With the Ones that stand above, it has begun moving.
With the White Rainbow it has begun moving.
With the Yellow-blossomed Plant it has begun moving.
With the Cornripener Beetle it has begun moving.
With the Long-life Happiness One it has begun moving.
    With the help of these it has begun moving.
    Now it has begun moving, now it has begun moving,
    Now it has begun moving, now it has begun moving.

3, 17, 33, 50. Song, *First Through Fourth Evenings*

>With these he is well again, with these he is well again,
>With these he is well again, with these he is well again.

With the Sons of Sun he is well again.
With the Sons of White Corn Boy he is well again.
With the Skin of Dark Cloud he is well again.
With the Flash of Lightning he is well again.
With the Skin of Black Wind he is well again.
With the Sound of Lightning he is well again.
With the Sons of the Long-life Happiness One he is well again.

>With these he is well again, with these he is well again,
>With these he is well again, with these he is well again.

With the Sons of Moon he is well again.
With the Sons of Yellow Corn Boy he is well again.
With Dark Cattails on top he is well again.
With the White Rainbow he is well again.
With Blue-blossom Pollen he is well again.
With the Sons of Cornripener he is well again.
With the Sons of the Long-life Happiness One he is well again.

>With these he is well again, with these he is well again,
>With these he is well again, with these he is well again.

18, 34, 51. Song, *Second Through Fourth Evenings*

>With these he walked, with these he walked,
>With these he walked, with these he walked.

With the Sons of White Corn Boy, with these he walked.
In the midst of Black Clouds, with these he walked.
In the midst of Lightning, with these he walked.
In the midst of Black Wind, with these he walked.
In the midst of Holy Lightning, with these he walked.
With the Sons of Long-life Happiness One, with these he walked.

>With these he walked, with these he walked,
>With these he walked, with these he walked.

With the Sons of Sun, with these he walked.
With the Sons of White Corn Girl, with these he walked.
In the midst of Lightning, with these he walked.
In the midst of Corn Pollen, with these he walked.
In the midst of Blue Corn Pollen, with these he walked.
In the midst of Cornripeners, with these he walked.
With the Sons of Long-life Happiness Ones, with these he walked.

>With these he walked, with these he walked,
>With these he walked, with these he walked.

19, 52. Song, Second and Fourth Evenings

With these he ran, with these he ran,
With these he ran, with these he ran.
With the Sons of Sun, with these he ran.
With the Sons of Yellow Corn Boy, with these he ran.
Among the Mountains, with these he ran.
In Flashes of Lightning, with these he ran.
In the Body of Black Wind, with these he ran.
In the midst of Thunders, with these he ran.
With the Sons of Long-life Happiness One, with these he ran.
With these he ran, with these he ran,
With these he ran, with these he ran.
With the Sons of Sun, with these he ran.
With the Sons of Yellow Corn Girl, with these he ran.
In Flashes of Lightning, with these he ran.
Among Rainbows, with these he ran.
In the Body of Blue Wind, with these he ran.
In the midst of Cornripeners, with these he ran.
With the Sons of Long-life Happiness One, with these he ran.
With these he ran, with these he ran,
With these he ran, with these he ran.

UNRAVELING

With the next song the practitioner rises and becomes active. He hands his rattle to a helper and, still singing, begins the unraveling procedures. He takes a *wooltááá* bundle in one hand; with his other hand he grasps the eagle feather which is fastened as a handle to the wound-around wool string. In this manner, with both hands, he presses the bundle against a significant portion of the patient's body. On the first evening two *wooltááá* bundles are used to loosen knots in the patient's feet. Two more bundles are applied, one to each of his arms. Finally, one bundle is destined for the point where back and neck run together. Chanting all the while, with one arm moving away from the patient in a sweeping motion, the singer then pulls the strings which are wound around the bundles. "The tight knots in the patient's body are so loosened."

The seven bundles on the second evening allow for additional applications on the breast and on the head. The nine bundles on the third night allow special attention for both knees. The eleven bundles on the fourth evening extend the realm of effectiveness to the outer points of the elbows.

On the first evening
two *wooltáá'd*
bundles are used to
loosen knots in the
patient's feet.

Two more bundles
are applied, one
to each of his arms.

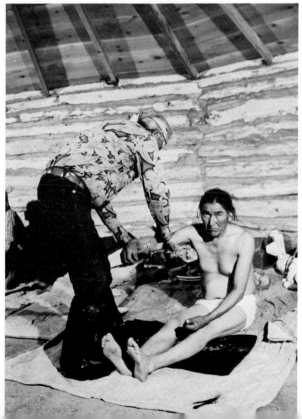

Finally, one bundle is destined for the point where back and neck run together.

Chanting all the while... the singer then pulls the strings which are wound around the bundles. "The tight knots in the patient's body are so loosened."

The seven bundles on the second evening allow for additional applications on the breast and on the head.

Loosening the tight knots of illness is only one of the objectives in the unraveling rite. The herbs in the *wooltáád* bundles contain significant and positive powers of health. Upon contact with the patient's skin, these powers begin to flow to the deficient places in his body where the knots have been loosened. As the bundle is unraveled, a quantity of herbal power is freed to enter the patient's body; it not only flows to deficient places but at the same time expels the agents of illness. The missiles or arrows of witchcraft are so loosened, displaced, and eventually removed. To assure the patient, as well as the gods who are present, that the unraveling has indeed been accomplished, the practitioner draws the handful of loosened strings over all the significant spots on the patient's body. The bundles themselves are taken outside and are disposed of at some distance from the hogan, together with the illness they have absorbed.

After the unraveling the patient is given *zaa'nił* to drink from a seashell—"the medicine to be put in the mouth." The "rub-on medicine," from the bowl, is applied to his body. All the while the group is chanting the song which narrates the first shaman's learning experience in the houses of the Coyote People. The two White, Yellow, Blue, and Black Coyote-persons, by whom he was led, we shall see later depicted in the sandpaintings. All references in this song to places

[45]

...the practitioner draws the handful of loosened strings over all
the significant spots on the patient's body.

...the patient is
given *zaa'nił* to
drink from a
seashell....

The "rub-on medicine," from the bowl, is applied to his body.

where the Holy People once walked relate also to the corresponding trails and places in the area where our ceremonial is now being performed:

4, 20, 35, 53. Song, *First Through Fourth Evenings*

By these he was led, by these he was led,
By these he was led, by these he was led.
By the Two White Ones who walk before you, by these he was led.
With the White Prayerstick in his hand, by these he was led.
Toward White Morning Dawn, by these he was led.
On the Trail toward the hogan, by these he was led.
On the Trail with the hogan in view, by these he was led.
On the Trail unto the hogan, by these he was led.
To the Walls of the hogan, by these he was led.
Near the Fire in the hogan, by these he was led.
Around the Fire in the hogan, by these he was led.
Into the Shadows of the hogan, by these he was led.
To a Corner in the hogan, by these he was led.
These are the places where they walked, by these he was led.
Happiness was given back to you, by these he was led.
These are the places where they walked, by these he was led.

[47]

Your name was given back to you, by these he was led.
Happiness was given back to you, by these he was led.
    By these he was led, by these he was led,
    By these he was led, by these he was led.

By the Two Yellow Ones who walk before you, by these he was lead.
With the Yellow Prayerstick in his hand, by these he was led.
Toward Yellow Evening....

By the Two Blue Ones who walk before you, by these he was led.
With the Blue Prayerstick in his hand, by these he was led.
Toward the Blue South....

By the Two Black Ones who walk before you, by these he was led.
With the Black Prayerstick in his hand, by these he was led.
Toward the Dark North....

BURNING THE FEATHERS

To conclude the Unraveling Ceremony, each evening a red-hot coal is laid before the patient. On this coal a mixture of plant powders and various feathers is sprinkled. From the rising smoke emanates a pungent smell; the patient rubs the smoke on his body. The plant powders are prepared from "the plant to which the birds fly" *(dehi dii'áii)*[3] and from a plant called "fire's sword" *(ko'bidiltł'ish)*. The feathers used are those of blue jay *(ch'ishii sháshii)*, bluebird *(joo'ish or dólii)*, and from the entire bird kingdom.

The Feather-burning Rite is used to conclude every ceremony in the entire nine-night ceremonial, except on the ninth night. Its purpose each time is the same. Luke Cook understands it thus: Formerly Coyote, when he ventured into Narrow Canyon, was shot full with the Bird People's feathery arrows. He became sick. After barely escaping to the rim of Narrow Canyon his kinsmen restored him by rubbing this same kind of feather-smoke on him. This measure charred and loosened the witchcraft arrows which had penetrated his body; they fell off and blew away (for the complete myth see Chapter 2).[4]

Later in this report will be printed a series of songs which link this mythic event to the patient's present predicament and cure. These songs are used during the Sweating portion of the Fire Ceremony on the third and fourth mornings. Their sequential numbers are 42

---

[3]Possibly Penstemon trichander.

[4]A parallel to this rite, the cure for a spider bite, is on record from Zuni: A tent is erected over the victim. Bluebird feathers are burned on hot coals. The smoke is inhaled, while the bite is treated with a mixture of water, coals, and burned feathers (Ladd 1960, p. 118). For mythological parallels see the section on "The Mythico-historical Origin of Coyoteway," Chapter 2.

From the rising smoke emanates a pungent smell; the patient
rubs the smoke on his body.

through 45, and 60 through 63. The Sweating Rite, which is part of the
Fire Ceremony and thus held during mornings, is, in fact, understood
as an amplified feather-removing procedure. Therefore, the con-
cluding song of the Sweating Rite on the fourth day, "They have blown
away" (Song 65), celebrates not only the accomplished results of
Sweating Rites but also of Feather-burning.

After feather-smoke is rubbed on the patient's body, the contami-
nated coal is extinguished with water and the ashes are carried outside,
together with the cornmeal from the symbolic "world of living minds."
Both remainders are deposited in the shadow of a living plant. Whatever powers of illness coal and cornmeal have absorbed in the course of
these exorcistic procedures, they are thus neutralized and banished.

For the duration of the Feather-burning Rite the singers rest. But
soon after the quenched coal is carried outside, all join to chant the
final song: "The sound was heard!" The sound of the departing agents
of illness—feathery arrows as they whizzed away—could be heard
throughout the known cosmos. The White, Yellow, Blue, and Black
Coyote People who live in the four directions of the underworld—
kinsmen—heard the whirring sound. The primeval healing process of
Coyote is reproduced as the ancient songs are sung once again, this
time in the surface world among humankind. This means that the
whirring sound was heard in all the known worlds concurrently. The

...all join to chant the final song: "The sound was heard!"

profane distinctions in space and time, of underworld and surface-world, of past and present, are exploded by this song. Human limitations become void, and so the patient emerges healthy from a new beginning.

Navajo healers are initiated, as happens to be the case with our patient, into the ways of divine origins. They learn to act out the archetypal roles of shamanic adventurers and patients. Contemporary patients are healed exactly in the same manner as the priestly practitioners have been initiated. Of this entire sacred history of preaccomplished facts the participants are aware when they repeat the divine songs at the appropriate moments in the ongoing history of Coyoteway. Presently they sing:

5, 21, 36, 54. Song, First Through Fourth Evenings

Hwii eiya eiya!
The sound was heard, the sound was heard.
The Son of the Two Rising heard the sound.[5]
The Early Morning Young Man heard the sound.

[5]Son of Sun and Moon as they rise in the east, White Coyote. Interestingly, Sun and Moon were said to be both masculine. By contrast, the Earth is feminine.

From the tail the sound was heard.
From the mouth the sound was heard.
From the tips of the fur the sound was heard.
The Yellow Kinsman heard the sound.
From the tip of the tongue the sound was heard.
The Blue Kinsman heard the sound.
From the tip of the tongue the sound was heard.
The Black Kinsman heard the sound.
   Happiness before you, the sound was heard.
   Happiness behind you, the sound was heard.

The Son of the Two Setting heard the sound.[6]
The Yellow Evening Sky heard the sound.
From the mouth the sound was heard.
From the tips of the gray fur the sound was heard.
The White Kinsman heard the sound.
From the tips of the fur the sound was heard.
The Blue Kinsman heard the sound.[7]
From the tip of the tongue the sound was heard.
The Black Kinsman heard the sound.[8]
From the tip of the tongue the sound was heard.
   Happiness behind you the sound was heard.
   Happiness before you the sound was heard.

The Son of the Two Above heard the sound.[9]
The Sunlight Young Man heard the sound.
From the tip of the tongue the sound was heard.
The White Kinsman heard the sound.
From the tips of the fur the sound was heard.
The Yellow Kinsman heard the sound.
From the tip of the tongue the sound was heard.
The Black Kinsman heard the sound.[10]
From the tip of the tongue the sound was heard.
Through the Streaks of Wind the sound was heard.
   Happiness before you, the sound was heard.
   Happiness behind you, the sound was heard.

The Son of Where the Stars Turn heard the sound.[11]

---

[6] Son of Sun and Moon as they set in the west, Yellow Coyote.

[7] On first day mistakenly sung as "Yellow Kinsman."

[8] On first day mistakenly sung as "Blue Kinsman."

[9] Son of Sun and Moon as they stand high in the south, Blue Coyote.

[10] On first day mistakenly sung as "Blue Kinsman."

[11] Son of the North, where Big Dipper turns around the Polar Star: Black Coyote.

The Dark Night Sky heard the sound.
From the tip of the tongue the sound was heard.
The White Kinsman heard the sound.
From the tips of the fur the sound was heard.
The Yellow Kinsman heard the sound.
From the tip of the tongue the sound was heard.
The Blue Kinsman heard the sound.
From the tip of the tongue the sound was heard.
Through the Streaks of Wind the sound was heard.
   Happiness behind you, the sound was heard.
   Happiness before you, the sound was heard.

"Blow away!" said the singer each evening as he concluded this song. On the first evening, being aware that he had made mistakes in the color sequence of the Kinsmen, and because he knew that he had confused a few lines, he humbly told Coyote: "I do not know your song, therefore I am saying this" *(niyiin doo bééhasingóó ádíshní).* What he may possibly have failed to accomplish because of his faulty singing he could achieve more directly, and perhaps as effectively, with his spoken command, "Blow away!"

Fire Ceremonies

The procedures on the first four mornings of the Coyoteway ceremonial are collectively called Fire Ceremonies *(kǫ' baa na'aldeehígíí)* or Rebuilding the Fire *(ach'i' déédíljah)*. Each of these four morning ceremonies features a ritual in which Reed-prayerstick Bundles *(lók'aa k'eet'áán násdizí)* are presented to various gods of the four directions. This procedure is followed each day by a Sweating Rite. The four mornings of dual rites begin on the first morning with Making New Fire. At the end of the fourth morning the Fire Ceremonies are concluded with a Washing Ritual.

Making New Fire

The old fire in the hogan is extinguished and the remains are carefully gathered and carried away. A dry piece of wood, cut from the soft stem of a century plant, is placed as bottom piece on a handful of shredded cedar bark. Notches are cut in the soft wood. Into these notches are trickled some grains from a lightning-struck rock *(tséghá-hindélii)*, not only to transfer to the wood the fire-producing power of lightning, but also "to increase friction." The drilling stick is made of some kind of hardwood; the species of the wood may be varied. The stick is twirled between the strong hands of two men, who take turns. But the wooden base refuses to glow for quite some time. All the while the singer chants the words which relate the present effort of making fire to the overall objective of healing:

6. Song, First Morning, Fire-making Song

By sternness, whatever your name is, the Firestick stands upright.[1]
By sternness, whatever your name is, the Firestick stands upright.
By Earth and Sky, and
    by sternness, whatever your name is, you are brought back.
By sternness, whatever your name is, the Firestick stands upright.
By the Long-life Happiness One, and
    by sternness, whatever your name is, you are brought back.
    By sternness, whatever your name is, the Firestick stands upright.
    By sternness, whatever your name is, you are brought back.

(This song may be repeated as often as is necessary until the fire burns; it ends as it begins with a repetition of the first line: "By sternness, whatever your name is, the Firestick stands upright.")

With all that effort in drilling and in singing, fire is still slow at coming forth. Unfavorable foreign influences are suspected as being the cause. A moratorium is put on my attempts in flash photography until there is fire. The patient's battery-powered lantern is also switched off. Quite obviously, the problem is a conflict between qualitatively different kinds of fire. Indeed, these measures succeed. New fire appears—sacred and pure fire, which is suited for the purification of a patient, of a hogan, and of all participants who take part in the ceremonial.

The Reed-prayerstick Bundle Rites

PREPARATIONS

The ritual of presenting Reed-prayerstick Bundles (lók'aa k'eet'áán násdizí) as offerings to various gods begins on the first morning immediately after the fire making. From the second through the fourth mornings preparations for the ritual are the first activity after awakening. Throughout the four mornings the rite remains quite uniform; it always begins with the same song, and it ends with a song that also remains the same. Four bundles are made on each of the first three days; only two bundles are needed on the fourth day. This variation is reflected in the prayers. They refer each day to different divine recipients of the offering bundles; only two deities are prayed to on the fourth day. Because the four Reed-prayerstick Bundle Rites are

---

[1]Sternness (hashké yił deeyá) means also "anger" and "severity."

The stick is twirled between the strong hands of two men, who take turns,
but the wooden base refuses to glow for quite some time.

New fire appears—sacred and pure fire....

The ritual of presenting Reed-prayerstick Bundles as offerings to various gods begins on the first morning immediately after the Fire Making.

nearly identical, I can discuss them here as one unit. The differences which by this method may appear from one day to the next do not interfere with the presentation.

Allowing for some flexibility when it is dictated by the scarcity of some materials, all offering bundles should, in addition to a Reed-prayerstick, contain six items: a feather of a blue jay *(ch'ishii sháshii)*, of a bluebird *(dólii)*, of an eagle *(átsá)*, of a turkey wing and beard *(tązhii, tązhii bé'ézhóó')*, together with a piece of cotton string *(ndik'ą')*. While the bundles are assembled, the divine recipients are addressed by a song:

7, 22, 37, 55. Song, First Through Fourth Mornings

I bring these to you, I bring these to you,
I bring these to you, I bring these to you.
Beautiful Things I bring to you.
Beautiful Songs I bring to you.
Under the Two Rising, I bring these to you.[2]
With the White One walking, I bring these to you,[2]
   the White Prayerstick I bring to you.

[2]These lines were omitted on the first morning. The song, as a whole, is very loosely structured.

Beautiful White Beads I bring to you.
Beautiful Feathers I bring to you.
Beautiful Tobacco I bring to you.[2]
Beautiful White Teeth I bring to you.
Beautiful White Salt I bring to you.
      I bring these to you, I bring these to you.
Beautiful Cornpollen I bring to you.
Your own Son I bring to you,
      the White Kinsman I bring to you,
      the White Prayerstick I bring to you.
Multi-colored Shells I bring to you.
Beautiful Feathers I bring to you.
Beautiful White Teeth I bring to you.
These things are beautiful.
      I bring these to you, I bring these to you,
      I bring these to you, I bring these to you.

A Tobacco Stick of the Two Setting I bring to you,
      the Yellow Prayerstick I bring to you.
The Yellow Cornpollen I bring to you.
Beautiful Feathers I bring to you.
Beautiful Teeth I bring to you.
Beautiful Things I bring to you,
Beautiful Things I bring to you.
Your own Son I bring to you,
      the Yellow Kinsman I bring to you,
      the Yellow Prayerstick I bring to you.
The Multi-colored Shell I bring to you.
Beautiful Feathers I bring to you.
Beautiful Teeth I bring to you.
      Beautiful Things I bring to you, Beautiful Things I bring to you,
      Beautiful Things I bring to you, Beautiful Things I bring to you.

A Tobacco Stick of the Two Above you I bring to you,
The Blue Prayerstick I bring to you.
Blue Turquoise Beads I bring to you.
Beautiful Feathers I bring to you.... (continued as in second stanza)

The Songs of the North I bring to you.
The Black Prayerstick I bring to you.
Beautiful Cornpollen I bring to you.
Beautiful Feathers I bring to you.... (continued as in second stanza)
      I bring these to you, I bring these to you,
      I bring these to you, I bring these to you.

...all offering bundles should, in addition to a Reed-prayerstick, contain six items.

While the bundles are assembled, the divine recipients are addressed by a song.

The Reed-prayerstick is the most important ingredient of the bundles. In fact, the offering bundles are named after it. With a traditional flint arrowhead a four-inch section is cut from the hollow stem of a common reed. The first ingredient of the stick is pollen; then it is stuffed with Navajo tobacco *(nát'oh waa'i)*—with white-blossomed, blue-blossomed, yellow-blossomed, and black-blossomed tobacco. Both ends of the prayerstick are then plugged with a paste made of water and pollen. Each stick is finally painted with the color that belongs to the direction for which it is intended—white for east, blue for south, yellow for west, and black for north. The colors and paints are obtained by grinding white bead *(yoołgaii)*, turquoise *(dootł'ishii)*, yellow abalone shell *(diichiłí)*, and jet *(bááshzhinii)*.

The Reed-prayerstick is actually intended to be a cigarette for the gods. Before it is put in the bundle it is "lighted" and made ready for the Holy Ones to smoke. For that purpose a quartz crystal is used to touch the tip of the prayerstick; fire from the sun is mediated by way of the quartz crystal.

From all this it would seem that the prayerstick is a very straightforward gift to the gods—a sort of friendly smoke between them and men. But this is not entirely so. Along with the various types of tobacco a small feather is smuggled inside. These cigarettes for the gods are loaded. The feathers represent the missiles of witchcraft. And so, while the Holy People enjoy and smoke their cigarettes, they unwittingly burn the arrows which have affected the patient. After the helper has finished his prayersticks he looks over his work. This gives him the idea of lighting a cigarette for himself. His smoke-stick is not loaded—it happens to be a King-size Salem which I have brought along.

Over all the contents in the offering bundles, before they are folded, a powdered mixture composed of the following ingredients is sprinkled: pollen from blue corn, from cattail reeds, from blue flowers, and from pine trees, along with powdered seaweeds, ocean foam, jewel dust, charcoal, and soil. After this, pollen is sprinkled toward the four directions and in a circle. The singer explains with a subdued voice the purpose of his action: "The offering bundles are blessed and become efficacious only with pollen." The blessings of pollen are also sprinkled on the patient; pollen is also put in the patient's mouth. Then the practitioner proceeds to fold the bundles and gives them to the patient to hold.

At this point in the preparations, on the first morning, some concern can be noted on the face of the leader. He suspects that somehow in the process the stack of offering bundles has been turned over and that the sequence is now confused. The bundles must be arranged in the sequence in which the prayers will be spoken; also, they must be arranged so that after the prayer they will be carried in the proper direction. To make sure that all is well with the bundles, they are opened once more to verify their destinations. The color of the prayer-sticks identifies each bundle for the directional deity for whom it is intended.

The plant bundles which lie ready on the floor (first through third mornings) are for the purification of the patient. In a similar manner as in the *wooltáád* ceremony on the evening before—except for the pulling of strings—the priestly practitioner touches his patient with plant bundles of four or five ingredients, chosen from among snake-weed *(ch'il diilyésii)*, blue grama grass *(tł'oh nástasí)*, Artemisia frigida *(tóyikááł)*, rock sagebrush *(ché'ézhííh)*, and spruce twigs *(ch'ó)*. On the fourth morning, however, the snow outside is so deep that the necessary plants can not be found; therefore the singer improvises and touches the patient with what he has available—the offering bundles. In any case, the patient is eventually given the Reed-prayerstick bundles to hold.

The first ingredient of the stick is pollen, then it is
stuffed with Navajo tobacco.

After the helper has finished his prayersticks he looks over his work.
This gives him the idea of lighting a cigarette for himself.

Over all the contents in the offering bundles, before they are folded,
a powdered mixture... is sprinkled....

After this, pollen is sprinkled toward the four directions and in a circle.

The blessings of pollen are also sprinkled on the patient....

...pollen is also put in the patient's mouth.

Then the practitioner proceeds to fold the bundles....

To make sure that all is well with the bundles they are opened
once more.... The plant bundles which lie ready on the floor are for the
purification of the patient.

On the fourth morning... the snow outside is so deep that the necessary
plants can not be found... therefore the singer improvises and touches the
patient with... the offering bundles.

PRAYERS

Holding the offering bundles, the patient repeats the prayers as
they are first spoken by the leader; in doing so he trails about a half
sentence behind his teacher. Each of the deities spoken to at the beginning of a prayer receives a bundle. On the second day, only, is each
bundle meant to be shared by two gods. The prayers for the first
morning are as follows:

8. Prayer, First Morning

Early Morning Shouting Young Man! (White Coyote)
From you I have the essences of life.
Today we smoke tobacco together.
Today you will remake my feet.
Today you will remake my legs.
Today you will remake my whole body.
Today you will remake my whole mind.
Today you will remake the sound of my voice.
Today the magic that is doing this removes it from me.
You will remove them from me.
You have removed them from me.
You are taking them far away from me.

Holding the offering bundles, the patient repeats the prayers
as they are first spoken by the leader....

They are far away from me.
Today I will be made well again.
Today I am not hurting anymore.
Today you have removed them from me.
The illness is moving.
It has moved out.
It is moving away from me.
You made me as well as I have been before.
I have been made well, as well as I have been before.
I am healthy now.
I am walking as before.
I am walking in health.
I am walking with a body free of fever.
I am walking with a light body.
I am walking with a perfect body.
I am walking with a body that is never to suffer again.
  Happiness is before me.
  Happiness is behind me.
The Long-life Happiness One, I am.
  All is Happiness.
  All is Happiness.

This prayer is repeated on the first day for Yellow Evening Young Woman (Shouting Yellow Coyote Woman), then for Sunbeam Young Man (Shouting Blue Coyote), then for Darkness Shouting Young Woman (Black Coyote Woman). The sequence "Happiness before me" and "Happiness behind me" is reversed with each successive prayer. Finally, the ending of the fourth prayer is more elaborate than the previous endings:

Happiness is behind me.
Happiness is before me.
Happiness is under me.
Happiness is above me.
Happiness is all around me.
With Yellow Cornpollen, from my mouth, Happiness will come.
The Long-life Happiness One, I am.
All is Happiness.
All is Happiness.

After these prayers, spoken to specific gods, follows what might be termed a "Prayer of Assurance." This prayer is identical on each of the four mornings, regardless of what deities are addressed in the preceding prayers.

According to these, Happiness will come to me from all places:
From the Flat Country, Happiness will come to me.
From the Plains, Happiness will come to me.
From the Thickets, Happiness will come to me.
From the Fogs, Happiness will come to me.
From the Hills, Happiness will come to me.
From the Gullies, Happiness will come to me.
From beneath Plants, Happiness will come to me.
From the Cornpollen path on which we walk,
*   Happiness will come to me.*
From Holy Places in the Earth, Happiness will come to me.
From our Dwellings, Cornpollen Houses, Happiness will come to me.
From out in the Woods, Happiness will come to me.
From beneath the Trees, Happiness will come to me.
From out of Canyons, Happiness will come to me.
From all red Canyons, Happiness will come to me.
From all black Canyons, Happiness will come to me.
From under the Rocks, Happiness will come to me.
From the Echoes of Canyon Walls, Happiness will come to me.
From stratified Rocks, Happiness will come to me.

From Cliffs, Happiness will come to me.
From Shrubs, Happiness will come to me.
From Places eroded by Water, Happiness will come to me.
From Valleys with Spruce Trees, Happiness will come to me.
From the Holy Mountains, Happiness will come to me.
From the House of Darkness, Happiness will come to me.
From the House of Early Morning, Happiness will come to me.
From the High Places, Happiness will come to me.
From where Sunlight strikes first, Happiness will come to me.
From Mountain Peaks, Happiness will come to me.
From the Sky, Happiness will come to me.
From Places beyond the Sky, Happiness will come to me.
From Places where White Wind walks, Happiness will come to me.
From Places where Yellow Wind walks, Happiness will come to me.
From Places where Blue Wind walks, Happiness will come to me.
From Places where Black Wind walks, Happiness will come to me.
From Places where the Sons of Wind are walking,
       Happiness will come to me.

I will walk in places where good Dark Clouds keep coming.
I will walk in places where good Male Rain keeps falling.
I will walk in places where benevolent Lightning keeps flashing.
I will walk in places where good Black Fog is moving.
I will walk in places where good Female Rain keeps falling.
I will walk in places where good Rainbows float about.
I will walk in places where good Thunders are rolling.
I will walk in places where I hear the Water Bird.
I will walk in places where on cliffs the Birds are heard.
I will walk in places where the good Yellow Bird is heard.
I will walk in places where the Cornripener Beetle is heard.
I will walk in places where chirps of good Young Birds are heard.
In places like these I will walk.
I will walk in places where every kind of Plant is growing.
I will walk in places where all sorts of Flowers are blooming.
I will walk among Dew and Pollen.
Pollen and Dew will touch my feet.
They will reach my legs.

By these the Breeze will blow through my hair.
By these the Breeze will penetrate my voice.
By these the Breeze will touch my sight.
By these the Breeze will enter my head.
By these the Breeze will affect my travels.

Happiness will come, behind me.
Happiness will come, before me.
Happiness will come, under me.
Happiness will come, above me.
Happiness will come, all around me.
With Cornpollen, Happiness will come from my mouth.
The Long-life Happiness One I am, walking.
All is Happiness.
All is Happiness.
All is Happiness.
All is Happiness.

The four prayerstick bundles on the second morning are each made for two deities—for a divine Wind and a divine Coyote-person. The content of the bundles is identical with those of the day before, except for additional diagonal stripes which are painted on the prayersticks. These stripes are the symbol of the Wind People. Accordingly, the formal prayers for presenting the offering bundles are repeated on the second day for White Wind and White Coyote in the east, for Yellow Wind and Yellow Coyote in the west, for Blue Wind and Blue Coyote in the south, and for Black Wind and Black Coyote in the north *(nítch'i* and *mą'ii łigaii, łitsooí, dootł'izhí, łizhiní).* (Prayer 23.)

On the third morning the four prayerstick bundles are given to Hidden Boy *(a yaaghá nilíní ashkii*—a Coyote), to White Dawn Girl *(bidah oogai at'ééd*—a Coyote Girl), to Flint Hill Boy *(béésh dah azk'idii ashkii*—a Coyote), and to Water Girl *(bił táálíní at'ééd*—a Coyote Girl). The formal prayers on that day, accordingly, are addressed to these deities (Prayer 38).

On the fourth and final morning of the Fire Ceremonies only two prayerstick bundles are made. They contain white and blue painted prayersticks. The white prayerstick bundle is for Talking-god *(hashch'éélti'í)* in the east; the blue one is for Calling-god *(hashch'éoghan)* in the south. Accordingly, only two prayers, plus the "Prayer of Assurance" are required for the last of the prayerstick bundle rites (Prayer 56).

In this manner, by the time fourteen prayerstick bundles have been delivered in the four directions, a total of eighteen gods have been contacted: Talking-god the chief of the Navajo pantheon and Calling-god, his closest helper; the four directional Wind People; and altogether twelve different Coyote-persons—the four Shouting Coyotes, the four Coyotes who are simply identified by their directional colors, together with Hidden Boy, White Dawn Girl, Flint Hill Boy, and Water Girl.

DELIVERY OF REED-PRAYERSTICK BUNDLES

On each of the first four mornings, after the formal prayers to the gods who are to receive the prayerstick bundles, the patient rises, circles the fire sunwise, and carries the bundles to their destinations, about one half mile in the four directions. As the patient rises, the singer folds the ground cloth which in the process has become his. The patient walks east and south; because of the severe snow a helper carries two bundles west and north for him. All bundles are deposited under a tree or under some other living plant. The appropriate opening phrases of the prayers which were spoken in the hogan are repeated when the bundles are deposited—to bring the matter again to the god's attention. On the fourth morning the two bundles which are made are taken east and south.

While the bundles are being carried outside, the singer in the hogan chants a song. On some days a few helpers remain to help him in the singing. The song that is being chanted recalls the adventures of the first shaman, when he walked with the four directional Coyote People, carrying prayersticks:

As the patient rises, the singer folds the ground cloth which
in the process has become his.

While the bundles are being carried outside, the singer
in the hogan chants a song.

On some days a few helpers remain to help him in the singing.

9, 24, 39, 57. *Song, First Through Fourth Mornings*

 He has walked.
Beneath the Two Rising before you, he has walked.
With White Morning Boy, he has walked.
With Corn-pollen at his feet, he has walked.
With the White Prayerstick in his hand, he has walked.
With Early Morning on him, he has walked.
With White Wind coming from his mouth, he has walked.
With Happiness before him, he has walked.
With Happiness behind him, he has walked.
 He has walked; he has walked;
  has walked, has walked, has walked, has walked.
Beneath the Two Setting before you, he has walked.
With Yellow Evening Girl, he has walked.
With Yellow Corn-pollen at his feet, he has walked.
With the Yellow Prayerstick in his hand, he has walked.
With Yellow Evening on him, he has walked.
With Yellow Wind coming from his mouth, he has walked.
With Happiness behind him, he has walked.
With Happiness before him, he has walked.
 He has walked; he has walked;
  has walked, has walked, has walked, has walked.
Beneath the Two Above you, he has walked.
With the Sunbeam Boy, he has walked.
With Corn-pollen at his feet, he has walked.
With the Blue Prayerstick in his hand, he has walked.
With Sunlight on him, he has walked.
With Blue Wind coming from his mouth, he has walked.
With Happiness before him, he has walked.
With Happiness behind him, he has walked.
 He has walked; he has walked;
  has walked, has walked, has walked, has walked.
Beneath Where-the-Stars-turn, he has walked.
With Darkness Girl, he has walked.
With Corn-pollen at his feet, he has walked.
With the Black Prayerstick in his hand, he has walked.
With Darkness on him, he has walked.
With Black Wind coming from his mouth, he has walked.
With Happiness behind him, he has walked.
With Happiness before him, he has walked.
 He has walked; he has walked;
  has walked, has walked, has walked, has walked.

After the song is finished, and when the bundle carriers have returned, the hogan is made ready for the next major portion of the Fire Ceremony. Firewood is carried inside for the Sweating Rite.

Sweating Rite

PREPARATIONS AND SWEATING

Together with the presentation of prayerstick bundles to directional gods, the ritual of sweating constitutes another major portion of the Fire Ceremonies. It is held on each of the first four mornings, always after the prayerstick bundles have been carried in the four directions.

Preparations for the Sweating Rite begin on the first evening with chopping *iiłkóóh* medicine. A coarse mixture of various plant materials, *iiłkóóh* consists of three groups of ingredients: twigs of trees and bushes, water plants, and portions of berry bushes. The twigs from trees and bushes are effective on the patient's skin—they are *ko' dahólóní,* "that which has fire." The six species used are greasewood

Preparations for the Sweating Rite begin already on the first evening with chopping *iiłkóóh* medicine.

(díwózhii), juniper *(gad)*, piñon *(deestsiin)*, prickly spruce and wide spruce *(ch'ó deinínii* and *teeł)*, and pine *(índíshchíí')*. A group of six water plants is aimed at affecting the patient's flesh. This group includes four kinds of reeds *(teeł, teeł nííyizí, teeł jik'ashí, teeł łikan)*, a plant the leaves of which look like arrowheads—possibly Brickellia grandiflora petiolaris *(tákáá' béésh)*, and algae *(tátł'id)*. Then finally, seven plants of a reddish color are added to affect the patient's blood. These are coyote berry—Forestiera neomexicana *(mạ'ii bidą́ą́')*, choke-cherry *(dzídzé)*, bitter berry *(dzídzé dík'ǫǫzhii)*, service berry *(dzídzé dit'ódi)*, turquoise berry *(dzídzé dootł'izhí)*, wild rose *(chxǫǫh)*, and something called *tichíí' yistání*. All put together and eventually boiled, *iiłkóóh* becomes a very strong tea; the flavors from the conifers dominate. *Iiłkóóh* medicine is intended to be an emetic.

For the Sweating Rite on each of the four mornings the regular fireplace, a converted oil drum with a stovepipe, is carried outside and a fire is built at the center of the hogan. Laid outward from the fire, in four directions, are four fire stirrers, each nearly a yard long. A juniper stick *(gad)* lies pointing east, a piñon stick *(deestsiin)* west, an oak stick *(chech'il)* south, and a scrub-oak stick *(chech'il ntł'izi)* pointing north.

Before the patient, that is, in a northwesterly direction from the fire, two features are being readied. A pile of sand is shaped in the form of a crater, as if to receive something. *Iiłkóóh* medicine is an emetic, and the patient later on explained the feature in terms of Coyote's vomiting. However, as far as I can presently see through the generally heavy smoke, our patient never vomits; neither do I nor does anybody else who drinks from the *iiłkóóh* brew. The crater of sand at any rate receives the solid remains of the rubbed-on *iiłkóóh* medicine. South of the sandpile a basket is placed in which medicines—first *iiłkóóh* for drinking and for rubbing-on, and later *kétłoh* for sprinkling—are prepared. *Iiłkóóh* medicine is first boiled in a large pot by the open fire. *Kétłoh* medicine, a dry mixture of plant materials, is simply sprinkled on *iiłkóóh* liquid in the basket. *Kétłoh* medicine used in the Sweating Rite is the same as that which has already been described for the Unraveling Ceremonies.

When all these things are in their proper places, all the participants disrobe, down to their shorts or breech cloths. Only men are present for this rite. The practitioner's modesty, faced with photographic equipment, is the reason why no pictures are taken during the sweating sessions. Tape-recording, sketching, and note-taking are, fortunately, all right. The shadow-drawing given here is based on notebook sketches, memory, and on previous photographic data.

When all these things are in their proper places, all the participants
disrobe, down to their shorts or breech cloths...the leader sings a song about
"the fur of the patient."

Then, as the flames shoot up toward the smoke-hole, and as the
smoke builds up to a nearly unbearable density (the new hogan is not
yet adequately ventilated), the leader sings a song about "the fur of the
patient"—which by way of ceremonial participation in the archetypal
mythical event is identical with the fur of Coyote. The white, yellow,
blue, and black water (*iiłkóóh* medicine) is presently boiling by the fire
to be eventually put on the "fur" of the patient—after that on the
"furs" of all the participants, including mine. The structure of the song
is simple—perhaps one of the oldest in the Coyoteway ceremonial:

10. Song, First Morning

This is the Fur, this is the Fur.
On the Tips of the Fur is the White Water.
On the Tips of the Fur is the White Medicine.
This is the Fur, this is the Fur.
On the Tips of the Fur is the Yellow Water.
On the Tips of the Fur is the Yellow Medicine.
This is the Fur, this is the Fur.
On the Tips of the Fur is the Blue Water.
On the Tips of the Fur is the Blue Medicine.
This is the Fur, this is the Fur.

On the Tips of the Fur is the Black Water.
On the Tips of the Fur is the Black Medicine.
  This is the Fur, this is the Fur.

  These are put on the Fur, these are put on the Fur.
The White Fur,
The White Water,
The White Medicine,
  This is the Fur, this is the Fur.
  These are put on the Fur, these are put on the Fur.
The Yellow Fur,
The Yellow Water,
The Yellow Medicine,
  This is the Fur, this is the Fur.
  These are put on the Fur, these are put on the Fur.
The Blue Fur,
The Blue Water,
The Blue Medicine,
  This is the Fur, this is the Fur.
  These are put on the Fur, these are put on the Fur.
The Black Fur,
The Black Water,
The Black Medicine,
  This is the Fur, this is the Fur.

  The Beautiful Fur, the Beautiful Fur.
The White Fur,
The White Water,
The White Medicine,

(Continued as in last stanza for Yellow Fur, Yellow Water, Yellow Medicine—then Blue, and Black)

The preparational song with which sweating is begun on the second morning (Song 25) is a variation of the first morning's opening song (Song 10). The Coyote-identification, where the patient's skin has become Coyote's fur, is now developed into a more complete Coyote mysticism. The ceremonial hogan, made of clay and logs, becomes a cosmic dwelling by virtue of its association with a complete set of directional colors. Moreover, the ceremonial hogan is now "in" the white, yellow, blue, and black Fur; that is to say, all participants are presently inside a Coyote-being of cosmic dimensions. The entire process of healing and initiation, even my recording, is accomplished in mystical union, literally "inside," the great Coyote.

25. Song, Second Morning

> This is the Hogan, this is the Hogan,
> This is the Hogan, this is the Hogan.

This is the Hogan given to me.
This is the White Clay Hogan.
This is the Hogan in the White Fur.
This is the Hogan that is immune.
This is the Hogan given to me.

> This is the Hogan, this is the Hogan,
> This is the Hogan, this is the Hogan.

This is the Hogan behind the Hill.
This is the Hogan in the Yellow Fur.
This is the Hogan of the Abalone Shell Lady.
This is the Hogan that is immune.
This is the Hogan built of Logs.

> This is the Hogan, this is the Hogan,
> This is the Hogan, this is the Hogan.

This is the Hogan built of Logs.
This is the Hogan in the Mountains.
This is the Hogan in the Blue Fur.
This is the Hogan that is immune.
This is the Hogan built of Logs.

> This is the Hogan, this is the Hogan,
> This is the Hogan, this is the Hogan.

This is the Hogan on top of the Mountain.
This is the Hogan in the Black Fur.
This is the Brown Hogan on top of the Mountain.
This is the Hogan that is immune.
This is the Hogan built of Logs.

> This is the Hogan, this is the Hogan,
> This is the Hogan, this is the Hogan.

This is the Hogan of your Son.
This is the Hogan that is immune.
This is the Hogan built of Logs.
This is the Hogan on top of the Mountain.
This is the Hogan of your Son.

> This is the Hogan, this is the Hogan,
> This is the Hogan, this is the Hogan.

Referring specifically to the seven reddish plant ingredients in the *iiłkóóh* brew, which are presently boiling by the fire, the priestly singer continues on the first morning with this song:

11. Song, First Morning

The Red Berry Shrubs are Medicine for my blood.
  They are Medicine, they are Medicine,
  They are Medicine, they are Medicine.
The Sons of these Medicines will help my blood.
  They will help, they will help,
  They will help, they will help.
The Sons of these Medicines are affecting my blood.
  They are affecting my blood, they are affecting my blood,
  They are affecting my blood, they are affecting my blood.

(This song is chanted four times.)

The next song depicts the setting of the timeless ceremonial; it refers to the first patient's recovery:

26. Song, Second Morning

  On these he walked, on these he walked,
  On these he walked, on these he walked.
  The Walking that is immune he walked.
On the White Grass he walked,
  the Walking that is immune he walked.
On the Blue Grass he walked,
  the Walking that is immune he walked.
On the Black Grass he walked,
  the Walking that is immune he walked.
On the Yellow Grass he walked,
  the Walking that is immune he walked.
  On these he walked.

  On the Ground he walked, on the Ground he walked,
  On the Ground he walked, on the Ground he walked.
On the White Ground he walked.
On the White Grass he walked.
The Walking that is immune he walked.
  On the Ground he walked, on the Ground he walked.

(The second stanza is repeated for Yellow Ground, Grass, Walking, then for Blue and Black. Song ends with four-fold refrain.)

The song which follows refers to the medicine which presently is being made—the *iiłkóóh* brew which boils by the fire:

27. Song, Second Morning

The Medicine is being made, the Medicine is being made,
The Medicine is being made, the Medicine is being made.
The Adulterous Coyote (mą'ii ałjiłnii) *is making the medicine.*
The Medicine is being made.
The Medicine he carries on his back.
The Medicine is being made.
The White Medicine,
The Medicine is being made.
The Holy Medicine,
The Medicine is being made.
Beneath the Two Rising,
The Medicine is being made.
The Medicine is being made, the Medicine is being made,
The Medicine is being made, the Medicine is being made.

The Staggering Coyote (atiin dooldisí) *is making the medicine.*
The Medicine is being made.
(Coming) from the Steep Places,
The Medicine is being made.
The Yellow Medicine,
The Medicine is being made.
The Holy Medicine,
The Medicine is being made.
Where the Two Above are setting,
The Medicine is being made.
The Medicine is being made, the Medicine is being made,
The Medicine is being made, the Medicine is being made.

The Badger (nahashch'id) *is making the medicine.*
The Medicine is being made.
(Coming) from the Dark Soil,
The Medicine is being made.
The Blue Medicine,
The Medicine is being made.
The Holy Medicine,
The Medicine is being made.
Beneath the Two Above,
The Medicine is being made.
The Medicine is being made, the Medicine is being made,
The Medicine is being made, the Medicine is being made.

The Gopher (na'azísí) *is making the Medicine.*
The Medicine is being made.

(Coming) from the Dark-brown Places,
  The Medicine is being made.
The Jet-black Medicine,
  The Medicine is being made.
The Holy Medicine,
  The Medicine is being made.
Where the Big Dipper turns,
  The Medicine is being made.
  The Medicine is being made, the Medicine is being made,
  The Medicine is being made, the Medicine is being made.

The preparational and sweating songs on the third and fourth mornings are identical. As before, the songs refer to the healing of the first Coyoteway patient. The references in the next two songs, to feathers and to feathers hanging down, will be better explained later on in Songs 42 through 45. Presently we join the patient as he is "walking out again," and as "he is walking in the water"—he and all those with him are sweating:

40, 58. Song, Third and Fourth Mornings

  With these, with these, he walked out again.
  With these, with these, he walked out again.
With a Stick, he walked out again.
With the Sun above him, he walked out again.
With the Waterbird People above him, he walked out again.
With this Medicine, he walked out again.
With this Feather, he walked out again.
With the White Feather hanging down, he walked out again.
With his Body, he walked out again.
  With these, with these he walked out again.
With these Feathers, he walked out again.
With the Sun above him, he walked out again.
With the Waterbird People above him, he walked out again.
With this Medicine, he walked out again.
With this Feather, he walked out again.
With these Feathers hanging down, he walked out again.
With his Body well, he walked out again.
  With these, with these, he walked out again.
  He is well.

41, 59. Song, Third and Fourth Mornings

  He is walking in the water, he is walking in the water,
  He is walking in the water, he is walking in the water.

With the Sun as his shield, he is walking in the water.
With these, he is walking in the water.
With the Heat People, he is walking in the water.
With the Sun as his shield, he is walking in the water.
With the Heat People, he is walking in the water.
With Feathers on his Head, he is walking in the water.
With Feathers hanging down, he is walking in the water.
With his Body shaking, he is walking in the water.
   He is walking in the water, he is walking in the water,
   He is walking in the water, he is walking in the water.
With being hot, he is walking in the water.
With the Sun as his shield, he is walking in the water.
With Feathers hanging down, he is walking in the water.
With Feathers hanging down, he is walking in the water.
With the White Feather, he is walking in the water.
With these, with these, he is walking in the water.
   He is walking in the water, he is walking in the water,
   He is walking in the water, he is walking in the water.

IIŁKÓÓH RUBBING-ON AND DRINKING

After the preparational sweating songs, the practitioner pours the boiling *iiłkóóh* brew from the pot into the basket near the patient. The patient then sifts the solids from the liquid by using a coarse brush; he rubs them on his body in such a manner that the rubbings fall into the sand hollow near the basket. Then he kneels and bows low to drink some of the liquid, directly from the basket. What he does not drink he rubs on his body. The other participants receive some of the liquid served in bowls—the singer drinks his portion directly from the dipper. While this takes place, on the first day, he chants three songs:

12. Song, First Morning

   It is his Water, it is his Water,
   It is his Water, it is his Water.
It is the White Medicine's Water.
It is the White Fur's Water.
It is the White Medicine's Water.
It is the Holy Medicine's Water.
   It is his Water, it is his Water,
   It is his Water, it is his Water.

(This stanza is repeated for Yellow, Blue, and Black. See Song 46 for a later variation.)

13. Song, First Morning

> *He who was given, lifts me by his hand.*
> *He who was given, lifts me by his hand.*
The White Fire-drill Bottom Piece, lifts me by his hand.
The White Medicine, lifts me by his hand.
The Holy Medicine, lifts me by his hand.
>> *These who were given, lift me by their hands.*
>> *These who were given, lift me by their hands.*
>> *These who were given, lift me by their hands.*
>> *These who were given, lift me by their hands.*

(This stanza is repeated for Yellow, Blue, and Black.)

14. Song, First Morning, same as Song 11

> *The Red Berry Shrubs are Medicine for my Blood....*

The songs which are chanted for *iiłkóóh* drinking and rubbing-on during the second Sweating Rite refer to the medicine which is now ready. The medicine will have been already sipped by the time the subsequent Song 29 is being chanted.

28. Song, Second Morning

> *The Medicine is ready, the Medicine is ready,*
> *The Medicine is ready, the Medicine is ready.*
The Adulterous Coyote has made the Medicine ready.
> *The Medicine is ready.*
Behind the Mountains where the trail goes,
> *The Medicine is ready.*
The White Medicine,
> *The Medicine is ready.*
The Holy Medicine,
> *The Medicine is ready.*
The Son of the Two Rising, it is he who has made the Medicine ready.
> *The Medicine is ready, the Medicine is ready,*
> *The Medicine is ready, the Medicine is ready.*
The Staggering Coyote has made the Medicine ready.
> *The Medicine is ready.*
(Coming) from the steep Slopes,
> *The Medicine is ready.*
The Yellow Medicine,
> *The Medicine is ready.*
The Holy Medicine,
> *The Medicine is ready.*

The Son of the Two Setting, it is he who made the Medicine ready.
  The Medicine is ready, the Medicine is ready,
  The Medicine is ready, the Medicine is ready.

(The next stanza is for Badger, the last stanza for Gopher—all after the pattern of Song 27.)

29. Song, Second Morning

  The Medicine I ate, the Medicine I ate,
  The Medicine I ate, the Medicine I ate.
The Adulterous Coyote has made the Medicine, the Medicine I ate.
Behind the Mountains where the trail goes, the Medicine I ate.
The White Medicine....

(All four stanzas are patterned after Song 28. Only the refrain is new.)

Then on the third and on the fourth mornings of the Sweating Rite, while *iiłkóóh* is being sipped, four songs celebrate the effects of this praiseworthy medicine. The feathery arrows of witchcraft are "coming out" from the patient's body; along with drops of sweat they are "dripping"; they are "falling"; and as a result of all these happenings—and as a result of the progression of these songs—the patient is made "well":

42, 60. Song, Third and Fourth Mornings

  With these, with these, it is coming out.
  With these, with these, it is coming out.
From the bones, it is coming out.
With the Sun as his shield, it is coming out.
With the Waterbird People above him, it is coming out.
With the Feathers hanging down, it is coming out.
With his body shaking, it is coming out.
With his body shaking, it is dripping.
With his body shaking, it is falling.
With his body shaking, he is well.
  With these, with these, it is coming out.
  With these, with these, it is coming out.
With the Heat, it is coming out.
With the Sun as his shield, it is coming out.
With the Waterbird People above him, it is coming out.
With the Feathers on his head, it is coming out.
With the White Feathers hanging down, it is coming out.
With his body shaking, it is coming out.
With his body shaking, it is dripping.

With his body shaking, it is falling.
With his body shaking, he is well.
   With these, with these, it is coming out.
   With these, with these, it is coming out.

43, 61. Song, Third and Fourth Mornings

   With these, with these, it is dripping.
   With these, with these, it is dripping.
With the Feathers falling, it is dripping.
With the Sun as his shield, it is dripping....
(Continued after the pattern of Song 42)

44, 62. Song, Third and Fourth Mornings

   With these, with these, it is falling.
   With these, with these, it is falling.
With the body shaking, it is falling.
With the Sun as his shield, it is falling....
(Continued after the pattern of Song 42)

45, 63. Song, Third and Fourth Mornings

   With these, with these, he is well.
   With these, with these, he is well.
With the Feathers falling, he is well.
With the Sun as his shield, he is well....
(Continued after the pattern of Song 42)

That some songs can be used to serve different purposes becomes evident if one examines the sequential scheme at the end of the third and the fourth day of sweating. Song 46, of the third day, is identical with Song 64 of the fourth day; however, while on the third morning it is chanted to complete the *iiłkóóh* rubbing, on the fourth morning it substitutes for the regular sprinkling song:

46, 64. Song, Third and Fourth Mornings

   It is his water, it is his water.
A White Coyote's water, it is his water.
The White Water he is walking in, it is his water.
The White Medicine, it is his water.
The Holy White Medicine, it is his water.
   It is his water, it is his water.

(This stanza is repeated for Yellow, Blue, and Black.)

The following song, like the previous one, is a variation of Song 12 and 13 with which actions were begun in the Sweating Rite on the first morning:

47. Song, Third Morning

He who was given lifts me in his hand.
He who was given lifts me in his hand.
The White Reed, lifts me in his hand.
The White Medicine, lifts me in his hand.
The Holy Medicine, lifts me in his hand.
He who was given lifts me in his hand.
He who was given lifts me in his hand.

(This stanza is repeated for Yellow, Blue, and Black.)

After the *iiłkóóh* medicine is properly applied, the patient rises, circles the fire sunwise, and goes outside. While he is absent, the helpers gather every trace of his *iiłkóóh* rubbings and the entire pile of sand. Together with the illness which has been captured there, these things are carried outside and disposed of at some distance. At this time also half of the fire is taken outside and deposited north of the hogan— further north on each successive morning. While these disease-absorbing elements are carried away, the patient waits outside; he keeps his distance to avoid catching the illness again. When he finally returns, the priestly singer prepares for sprinkling the participants with *kétłoh* medicine.

SPRINKLING *KÉTŁOH*

Every Sweating Rite includes sprinkling of *kétłoh* medicine—the same rub-on medicine which has been described in connection with the Unraveling Ceremonies. The practitioner pours the remaining *iiłkóóh* liquid from the pot by the fire into his basket. To the liquid he adds *kétłoh* powder. With a bundle of large eagle feathers, and with a song, the priest begins sprinkling the wholesome contents of the basket first on the patient, then on every participant around the circle, sunwise. I happen to sit on the south side and am therefore the first of the participants to get showered. On the first day I dodge the liquid to protect my recording equipment—the singer laughs out loud, nearly interrupting his song. His sport from here on out is to aim his load straight at my face. On the second day I know what to expect; I quietly cover my equipment and solemnly present my face to his showers of blessings. He is surprised, even takes a second look to reassure himself. I have the feeling that he respects me for it. The next round is sprinkled more generally for the cardinal directions. Last to be blessed is the practitioner's own pad and his equipment.

The words of the sprinkling song are quite significant in this procedure. On the fourth morning the singer sprinkles to Song 64, "It is his water" (same as Song 46 above). The liquid medicines which are used in any rite of the Coyoteway ceremonial are Coyote's water. The idea of getting blessed by Coyote's water is carried one step further in the sprinkling song which is used on the first three mornings. According to this song, the furs which "are put in the water"—are being sprinkled—are the coyote furs of the patient and of all the participants. All of us participate, ceremonially, in a fully developed Coyote mysticism. And here is the song:

15, 30, 48. Song, First Through Third Mornings

The Furs are put in the water.
Black Lightning is put in the body.
Male Rain is there.
Black Water is there.
Crystal Rock is there.
In the wide Land I walk.

The Black Fur is put in the rainbow.
It is put in the Black Water.
The White Crystal is there.
Roads to the wide Land I walk.
The Holy Black Cloud is there.
Crystal Rock is there.
In the Black Water I walk.

To the Beautiful Place I walk.
In the Country of Water I walk.
Furs put into Corn-pollen,
And beautiful Water is there.

BURNING THE FEATHERS

Every major ceremony in the Coyoteway ceremonial, except the ninth night, concludes with the act of burning the feathers. The procedure and the meaning are always the same. Arrows of witchcraft —bird feathers shot into the primeval Coyote skin—are burned, removed, and blown far away from the patient. The fiery coal, again, is drenched with water and carried outside with some of the illness adhering to it. The Feather-burning Rite is generally a silent procedure. Only at the end of the fourth Sweating Rite is it accompanied by a song. Structurally this song is a continuation of Songs 42 through 45 (same as 60 through 63). The song recognizes the accomplished fact of the exorcistic process which in Song 5, the song following feather-burning in the Unraveling Ceremony, is still going on. Now the witchcraft feathers are not only heard whizzing away; now it is certain that "they have blown far away."

65. Song, Fourth Morning

> They have blown far away, they have blown far away,
> They have blown far away, they have blown far away.
> With the Sun as your shield, they have blown far away.
> With the Hardwood Shrub People (burning),
>   they have blown far away.
> With the Bird People above, they have blown far away.
> With the Ones that stand above, they have blown far away.
>   With these you are made well, with these you are made well,
>   With these you are made well, with these you are made well.
> With the Bear People, they have blown far away.
> With the Sun as your shield, they have blown far away.
> With all Furry People, they have blown far away.
> With the body shaking, it is coming out.
> With the body shaking, it is dripping.
> With the body shaking, it is falling.
> With the body shaking, you are made well.
>   They have blown far away, they have blown far away,
>   They have blown far away, they have blown far away.

The Washing Rite

The four Fire Ceremonies are concluded on the fourth morning with the Washing Rite. An open fire burns at the center of the hogan. A bucket load of sand is brought in and put between the fire and the patient. The sand is leveled. Spruce twigs are laid on the sand; snake-weed and other grasses—the same as are in the *wooltáád* bundles—are laid on the spruce twigs. Finally, a basket is set on top of these. Hot water is poured into the basket, and while the patient undresses, the singer works up a lather by wringing yucca leaves. The patient circles the fire, sunwise. On the white yucca suds, in the basket, the practitioner sprinkles greenish *kétłoh* powder in the shape of the familiar circle, with the four directional lines leading out from the center.

Then the patient kneels to face the basket; the singer loosens the man's hair. The hair is washed in the yucca suds. After the hair the entire body is cleansed. The remains of this procedure—spilled suds, sand, and the disease-absorbing plants—are all carried outside. The act of washing, up to this point, has obviously been an exorcistic rite of purification. The song which is chanted to accompany the washing, however, dwells on the positive aspect: since mythical times, by the efforts of Coyoteway singers, health, long life, and happiness were "brought back."

66. Song, Fourth Morning

> He brought it back, he brought it back,
> He brought it back, he brought it back.
> With these he brought it back.
> The Sons of Sun, with these he brought it back....
> (This song is the same as Song 31.)

Water cleanses from dirt and even washes away the exorcized missiles of witchcraft. It cleanses and removes, but it does not replenish the vacuum which in this process of healing is created. Therefore, immediately after the washing, the patient's hair, face, and body are infused with new life-power through the application of cornmeal.

An open fire burns at the center.... A bucket load of sand...
between the fire and the patient... is leveled.

Spruce twigs are laid on the sand; snakeweed and other grasses...
are laid on the spruce twigs.

Hot water is poured into the basket... the singer works up
a lather by wringing yucca leaves.

On the white yucca suds… the practitioner sprinkles greenish *kétłoh* powder in the shape of the familiar circle, with the four directional lines leading out from the center.

Then the patient kneels to face the basket; the singer loosens the man's hair.

His hair is washed in yucca suds.

After a while the patient continues applying the cornmeal by himself. He also puts cornmeal on his clothes. This, surely, is no longer purification, but rather an addition of positive powers. Meanwhile, the singer chants a song—variations on Song 2. The modifications are noteworthy. The exorcistic implications of the original Song 2—"Now it has begun moving"—are replaced here by a direct reference to the patient's ability to move and to walk about in health:

67. Song, Fourth Morning

Now he is moving, now he is moving,
Now he is moving, now he is moving.
With the help of these he is moving:
With the Sons of Sun, he is moving.
With the Sons of White Corn Girl, he is moving.
With Dark Cattails on top, he is moving.
With the Flash of Lightning, he is moving.
With the Black-blossomed Plant, he is moving.
With the Sound of Lightning, he is moving.
With the Long-life Happiness One, he is moving.
Now he is moving, now he is moving,
Now he is moving, now he is moving.

[91]

After the hair the entire body is cleansed.

...the patient's hair, face, and body are therefore infused with new life-power through the application of cornmeal.

With the Sons of Moon, he is moving.
With the Sons of Yellow Corn, he is moving.
With Dark Cattails on top, he is moving.
With the White Rainbow, he is moving.
With the Yellow-blossomed Plant, he is moving.
With the Corn-ripener Beetle, he is moving.
With the Long-life Happiness One, he is moving.
    Now he is moving, now he is moving,
    Now he is moving, now he is moving.

68. Song, Fourth Morning

    Now he is walking, now he is walking,
    Now he is walking, now he is walking.
    With the help of these he is walking:
With the Sons of Sun, he is walking....
(Sung after the pattern of Song 67.)

After these songs the practitioner blesses the patient with pollen; he puts some pollen into the patient's mouth, then some on his head. Then he sprinkles pollen in the four directions and explains: "The suds of yucca alone do not heal a person. When the blessings of cornpollen are added, real renewal takes place." Now a pollen bag is passed so that all of us can obtain the same blessings. In the end the singer sprinkles pollen on his paraphernalia and gets ready to sing again.

After pollen-sprinkling the thematic progression of Songs 66 through 68—"He brought it back," "Now he is moving," "Now he is walking"—is continued in two more songs. In these final songs the patient is no longer referred to in third person singular; rather, he now exclaims in first person singular "It is I walking!" and "It is I made strong!" He no longer sees himself as a shadow-figure in the trail of that first Coyoteway patient and shaman; he now *is* that first patient and shaman.

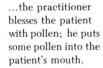

69. Song, Fourth Morning

> *It is I, it is I walking!*
> *It is I, it is I walking!*
> *It is I, it is I walking!*
> *It is I, it is I walking!*
> *The White Corn Boy, it is I walking.*
> *Beneath the Two Rising, on White Mountain, it is I walking.*

...the practitioner blesses the patient with pollen; he puts some pollen into the patient's mouth.

Then he sprinkles pollen in the four directions and explains....

With Pollen, it is I walking.
Happiness before me, it is I walking.
Happiness behind me, it is I walking.
   It is I, it is I walking!
   It is I, it is I walking!
   It is I, it is I walking!
   It is I, it is I walking!

The Yellow Corn Boy, it is I walking.
Beneath the Two Setting, on Yellow Mountain, it is I walking....
(continued as in first stanza)

The Blue Corn, it is I walking.
Beneath the Two, on Blue Mountain, it is I walking....
(continued as in first stanza)

The Black Corn, it is I walking.
Beneath where Big Dipper turns, it is I walking....
(continued as in first stanza)

70. Song, Fourth Morning

   It is I, it is I made strong!
   It is I, it is I made strong!

It is I, it is I made strong!
It is I, it is I made strong!
The White Corn Boy, it is I made strong....
(continued after the pattern of Song 69)

These songs conclude the Washing Rite, the Fire Ceremonies, and so the first four days of the Coyoteway ceremonial. This is the end of the fourth morning. Tonight, on the fifth evening of the ceremonial, the Basket-drum Singing will begin.

Basket-Drum Ceremonies

PREPARATIONS AND AIM

Songs are chanted to the accompaniment of a basket-drum from the fifth through the eighth evenings of the Coyoteway ceremonial. As before, most of these songs refer to the performance of the first Coyoteway ceremonial and to the archetypal Coyote People. Coyote has been the first sufferer, the first who was healed by Coyoteway, and also the first to teach his healing procedures to human apprentices. Health, well-being, and general blessings emanate therefore from the Coyote People whose presence in the surface world is realized by singing their own archaic and proven songs.

The basket-drum songs on the fifth evening actually begin a new type of ceremony which in each instance climaxes on the next morning in the appearance of a masked *yé'ii*-impersonator. For three days in a row a blue-masked god from the underworld visits the patient. On the last day as many as three *yé'ii*-impersonators appear in answer to the previous night's basket-drum songs.

Two large leaves of a yucca plant are knitted together into a drumstick with slices of yucca leaves. Kernels of maize are wrapped into the drumstick—one for each participating member. Before him the practitioner sprinkles a leveled spot with cornmeal. Then, at that same place a moistened wedding basket is placed upside down on one side of a blanket. The remaining portion of the blanket is folded over the basket; the basket-drum is ready for use.

The participants sit in a circle around the singer. The patient sits at his regular place north of the practitioner. While the helpers sing along and take turns among each other with the rattle, the practitioner beats the drum and leads in the singing. After the first song the patient goes briefly outside; he reenters to sit somewhere along the southside of the hogan. This is done to separate him from the old place with which his illness has become associated. Moreover, the group of people, chanting blessing songs, form a human shield charged with divine song power to protect the patient from his former troubles.

FIFTH EVENING

The following basket-drum songs are chanted in unison on the fifth evening of the Coyoteway ceremonial:

71. Song, Fifth Evening

This is the Fur, this is the Fur.
On the Tips of the Fur is the White Water.
On the Tips of the Fur is the White Medicine....
(This song is the same as Song 10.)

Two large leaves
of a yucca plant are
knitted together
into a drumstick
with slices of yucca
leaves.

While the helpers sing along and take turns among each other with the rattle, the practitioner beats the drum and leads in the singing.

...the group of people, chanting blessing songs, form a human shield charged with divine song power to protect the patient from his former troubles.

72. Song, Fifth Evening, similar to Song 25

This is the Hogan, this is the Hogan,
This is the Hogan, this is the Hogan.
This is the Hogan given to me.
This is the White Clay Hogan.
This is the Hogan in the White Fur.
This is the Hogan that is immune.
This is the Hogan given to me.
This is the Hogan, this is the Hogan,
This is the Hogan, this is the Hogan.
This is the Hogan built of Logs.
This is the Hogan in the Mountains
This is the Hogan in the Blue Fur.
This is the Hogan that is immune.
This is the Hogan built of Logs.
This is the Hogan, this is the Hogan,
This is the Hogan, this is the Hogan.
This is the Hogan behind the Hill.
This is the Hogan of the Abalone Shell Lady.
This is the Hogan in the Yellow Fur.
This is the Hogan that is immune.
This is the Hogan behind the Hill.
This is the Hogan, this is the Hogan,
This is the Hogan, this is the Hogan.
This is the Hogan on top of the Mountain.
This is the Brown Hogan on the Mountain.
This is the Hogan in the Black Fur.
This is the Hogan that is immune.
This is the Hogan on top of the Mountain.
This is the Hogan, this is the Hogan,
This is the Hogan, this is the Hogan.
With these he is made well again, with these he is made well again,
With these he is made well again, with these he is made well again.

Song 72 is a reduced version of Song 25. It is reduced to four stanzas to accommodate the four directional colors—white (east), blue (south), yellow (west), black (north). Song 72 is repeated three times with sequential variations—south, west, north, east; west, north, east, south; north, east, south, west.

73. Song, Fifth Evening

With their Blood in me I am immune,
With their Blood in me I am immune,

With their Blood in me I am immune,
With their Blood in me I am immune.
With the Wind People's Blood in me,
With the Corn-ripener Beetle's Blood in me,
With the White Medicine's Blood in me,
With the Corn-ripener Sons' Blood in me,
    With their Blood in me I am immune.
With the Blue Sky in me,
With the Sons of Blue Sky in me,
With the White Medicine in me,
    With their Blood in me I am immune.
With the Yellow Medicine in me,
With the White Medicine in me,
    With their Blood in me I am immune,
    With their Blood in me I am immune,
    With their Blood in me I am immune,
    With their Blood in me I am immune.

74. Song, Fifth Evening

Down the Mountain, they roll it over him.
Down the Mountain, they roll it over him.
Down the Mountain, they roll it over him.
Down the Mountain, they roll it over him.
The Rock of Black Cloud's Sons, they roll it over him.
The Rock of White Medicine, they roll it over him.
I am immune, they roll it over him.
It is their Rock, they roll it over him.
The Blue Lizards' Rock, they roll it over him.
At the Place of Yellow Evening, they roll it over him.
The White Medicine's Rock, they roll it over him.
I am immune, they roll it over him.
    Down the Mountain, they roll it over him.
    Down the Mountain, they roll it over him.
    Down the Mountain, they roll it over him.
    Down the Mountain, they roll it over him.

Song 74 refers to the episode mentioned in the myth by *tséyi'nii*
(Chapter 10): Coyote came to a place where lizards were sliding down
on rocks. He wanted to slide down with them, but a rock fell on him
and smashed him. The song implies that the lizards rolled a rock over
him. According to the myth, Coyote survived and recovered; this is the
important point for the present healing effort. Together with Coyote,
even with rocks crashing on him, the patient is considered immune.

The next two songs elaborate on the Coyote mysticism according to which the patient and the tenacious Coyote are one.

75. Song, Fifth Evening

He has come back and I am walking, as I am walking with him.
With his Body I am walking, as I am walking with him.
On the Path I am walking, as I am walking with him.
With his Body I am walking, as I am walking with him.
  My Body is immune as I am walking, as I am walking with him.
With the Fur I am walking, as I am walking with him.
  My Body is immune as I am walking, as I am walking with him.
In the Woods I am walking, as I am walking with him.
  My Body is immune as I am walking, as I am walking with him.
With the Black Fur I am walking, as I am walking with him.
  My Body is immune as I am walking, as I am walking with him.
On the Path to Water I am walking, as I am walking with him.
  My Body is immune as I am walking, as I am walking with him.
I am not ashamed as I am walking, as I am walking with him.
  My Body is immune as I am walking, as I am walking with him.
I am not ashamed as I am walking, as I am walking with him.

76. Song, Fifth Evening

I am not ashamed as I am walking, as I am walking with him.
I am not ashamed as I am walking, as I am walking with him.
I am not ashamed as I am walking, as I am walking with him.
I am not ashamed as I am walking, as I am walking with him.
In the White Fur I am walking, as I am walking with him.
The Path behind the Hill I am walking, as I am walking with him.
  My Body is immune as I am walking, as I am walking with him.
On the Path to Water I am walking, as I am walking with him.
With the Medicine I am walking, as I am walking with him.
  My Body is immune as I am walking, as I am walking with him.

In the Blue Fur I am walking, as I am walking with him.
With the White Corn I am walking, as I am walking with him.
  My Body is immune as I am walking, as I am walking with him....
(continued as in first stanza)

In the Yellow Fur I am walking, as I am walking with him.
The Path behind the Hill I am walking, as I am walking with him.
  My Body is immune as I am walking, as I am walking with him.
(continued as in first stanza)

In the Black Fur I am walking, as I am walking with him.

With the White Corn I am walking, as I am walking with him.
My Body is immune as I am walking, as I am walking with him....
(continued as in first stanza)
I am not ashamed as I am walking, as I am walking with him.
I am not ashamed as I am walking, as I am walking with him.
I am not ashamed as I am walking, as I am walking with him.
I am not ashamed as I am walking, as I am walking with him.

77. Song, Fifth Evening

Hogan below from where he emerges,
Hogan below from where he comes out in a circle,
Hogan below from where he comes out in a circle.
Long Hogan from where he emerges.
Hogan made of White Fur, made in a circle.
Under the Rocks from where he emerges.
My Body is made immune, made in a circle.
Hogan below from where he comes out in a circle,
Hogan below from where he comes out in a circle.
Long Hogan from where he emerges.
Hogan made of Blue Fur, made in a circle.
(Continued as in first stanza. Third and fourth stanzas are sung with
Yellow Fur and Black Fur respectively.)

Song 77 presents an interesting, and very logical, mixture of Pueblo
Indian emergence mythology and Apachean hunter wit. The hole of
emergence is here a foxhole (foxes are coyotes) under a rock. The
underworld hogan of Coyote is recognized as a long underground
burrow, extending in a circle.

78. Song, Fifth Evening

The Adulterous Coyote, he walks underground.
The Song he sings does not affect me, he walks underground.
In the White Fur, he walks underground.
A Song he sings, as he walks underground.
The Song he sings does not affect me, he walks underground.
He does not see me, as he walks underground.
He sings under a Spruce Tree, as he walks underground.
The Song he sings does not affect me, he walks underground.
The Sunset Twilight Boy, he walks underground.
The Song he sings does not affect me, he walks underground.
He sings under a Spruce Tree, as he walks underground.
The Song he sings does not affect me, he walks underground.

79. Song, Fifth Evening

The Adulterous Coyote, he calls everywhere, underground.[1]
A Song he sings, he calls everywhere, underground.
The Song he sings does not affect me,
    he calls everywhere, underground.
The One Running Along the Path, under the Spruce Tree,
    he calls everywhere, underground.
The Song he sings does not affect me,
    he calls everywhere, underground.
The One Running Along the Path, under the Spruce Tree,
    he calls everywhere, underground.
The Song he sings does not affect me,
    he calls everywhere, underground.

The One Running Along the Path, on the Rock,
    he calls everywhere, underground.

80. Song, Fifth Evening

    He makes the Medicine, he makes the Medicine,
    He makes the Medicine, he makes the Medicine,
    He makes the Medicine, he makes the Medicine,
    He makes the Medicine, he makes the Medicine.
The Adulterous Coyote, he makes the Medicine.
Below the Cliffs, he makes the Medicine.
The White Fur, he makes the Medicine.
The Holy Medicine, he makes the Medicine.
    The Making of the Medicine, he makes the Medicine.
Out among the Hills, he makes the Medicine.
The Holy Medicine, he makes the Medicine.
The Crystal Medicine, he makes the Medicine.
The Holy Medicine, he makes the Medicine.
    The Making of the Medicine, he makes the Medicine.

81. Song, Fifth Evening

    I put it in your mouth, I put it in your mouth,
    I put it in your mouth, I put it in your mouth.
The Black Medicine, I put it in your mouth.
The Invisible Medicine, I put it in your mouth.
The White Medicine, I put it in your mouth.
The Holy Medicine, I put it in your mouth.
The Invisible Medicine, I put it in your mouth.

---

[1]Literally "he does everything"—explained by the singer as "he calls everywhere."

The White Corn, I put it in your mouth.
The Yellow Medicine, I put it in your mouth.
The Holy Medicine, I put it in your mouth.
The Invisible Medicine, I put it in your mouth.
The Evening Yellow, I put it in your mouth.
The Blue Medicine, I put it in your mouth.
The Holy Medicine, I put it in your mouth.
The Invisible Medicine, I put it in your mouth.
The Crystal Medicine, I put it in your mouth.
The Holy Medicine, I put it in your mouth.
The Medicine is holy to him.
> I put it in your mouth, I put it in your mouth,
> I put it in your mouth, I put it in your mouth.

82. Song, Fifth Evening

> I put it in your mouth, he is eating it;
> for its miraculous power, he is eating it,
> for its miraculous power, he is eating it.

The White Medicine, he is eating it.
The Holy Medicine, he is eating it.
Here the Medicine, he is eating it.
The Holy Medicine, he is eating it.
Here the Medicine, he is eating it.
For its miraculous power, he is eating it.
The Crystal Medicine, he is eating it.
The Holy Medicine, he is eating it.
Here the Medicine, he is eating it.
> I put it in your mouth, he is eating it:
> for its miraculous power, he is eating it,
> for its miraculous power, he is eating it.

83. Song, Fifth Evening

> The Hawks are going in pairs, the Hawks are going in pairs,
> The Hawks are going in pairs, the Hawks are going in pairs.
Out on the Plains they are going in pairs.
On a Path behind the Ridge they are going in pairs.
> (To their feathery arrows) I am immune.

(This stanza is sung four times.)

84. Song, Fifth Evening

> The Pairs keep going behind ridges,
> The Pairs keep going behind ridges,

The Pairs keep going behind ridges,
The Pairs keep going behind ridges.
White Coyote Pairs keep going behind ridges.
Black Coyote Pairs keep going behind ridges.
The White Medicine, they are eating it.
The Black Medicine, they are eating it.
    I am immune.
    The Pairs keep going behind ridges,
    The Pairs keep going behind ridges,
    The Pairs keep going behind ridges,
    The Pairs keep going behind ridges.
Yellow Coyote Pairs keep going behind ridges.
Blue Coyote Pairs keep going behind ridges.
The Yellow Medicine, they are eating it.
The Blue Medicine, they are eating it.
    I am immune.
    The Pairs keep going behind ridges,
    The Pairs keep going behind ridges,
    The Pairs keep going behind ridges,
    The Pairs keep going behind ridges.

85. Song, Fifth Evening

    He carried it away, far away, he carried it away.
    He carried it away, far away, he carried it away.
Beneath the Two Rising, he carried it away.
The White Prayerstick in his hand, he (White Coyote) carried it away.
With Happiness before him, he carried it away.
With Happiness behind him, he carried it away.
    He carried it away, far away, he carried it away.
    He carried it away, far away, he carried it away.
Beneath the Two Above, he carried it away.
The Blue Prayerstick in his hand, he (Blue Coyote) carried it away.
With Happiness behind him, he carried it away.
With Happiness before him, he carried it away.
    He carried it away, far away, he carried it away.
    He carried it away, far away, he carried it away.
Beneath the Two Setting, he carried it away.
The Yellow Prayerstick in his hand,
    he (Yellow Coyote) carried it away....
(continued as in first stanza)
    He carried it away, far away, he carried it away.
    He carried it away, far away, he carried it away.
Beneath Where the Stars Turn, he carried it away.

The Black Prayerstick in his hand,
    he (Black Coyote) carried it away....
(continued as in second stanza)
        He carried it away, far away, he carried it away.
        He carried it away, far away, he carried it away.

SIXTH EVENING

The following basket-drum songs are chanted in unison on the sixth evening of the Coyoteway ceremonial:

89. Song, Sixth Evening

    To the Hogan I came, to the Hogan I came,
    To the Hogan I came, to the Hogan I came.
Beneath the Two Rising, to the Hogan I came.
To the Hogan of White Coyote, to the Hogan I came.
Round Corn across the Door, to the Hogan I came.
On the Pollen-path I came, to the Hogan I came.
Sunshine over the Door, to the Hogan I came.
To the Holy Hogan, to the Hogan I came.
    To the Hogan I came, to the Hogan I came,
    To the Hogan I came, to the Hogan I came.
Beneath the Two Above, to the Hogan I came.
To the Hogan of Blue Coyote, to the Hogan I came.
(continued as in first stanza)
    To the Hogan I came, to the Hogan I came,
    To the Hogan I came, to the Hogan I came.
Beneath the Two Setting, to the Hogan I came.
To the Hogan of the Yellow Coyote, to the Hogan I came.
(continued as in first stanza)
    To the Hogan I came, to the Hogan I came,
    To the Hogan I came, to the Hogan I came.
Beneath Where the Stars Turn, to the Hogan I came.
To the Hogan of the Black Coyote, to the Hogan I came.
(continued as in first stanza)
    To the Hogan I came, to the Hogan I came,
    To the Hogan I came, to the Hogan I came.

Referring again to all the four directions, this song is repeated three times. The second round is sung by beginning with south (Beneath the Two) and with Blue Coyote. The third round begins with west (Beneath the Two Setting) and the Yellow Coyote. The fourth round begins with north (Where the Stars Turn) and ends with west.

90. Song, Sixth Evening

It is I, it is I walking!
It is I, it is I walking!
It is I, it is I walking!
It is I, it is I walking!
The White Corn Boy, it is I walking....
(This song is the same as Song 69.)

91. Song, Sixth Evening

I caught up with him, I caught up with him,
I caught up with him, I caught up with him.
Beneath the Two Rising, I caught up with him.
(White Coyote) With the White Prayerstick in his hand,
I caught up with him.
With Happiness before me, I caught up with him.
With Happiness behind me, I caught up with him.
I caught up with him, I caught up with him,
I caught up with him, I caught up with him.
Beneath the Two Above, I caught up with him.
(Blue Coyote) With the Blue Prayerstick in his hand,
I caught up with him.
With Happiness behind me, I caught up with him.
With Happiness before me, I caught up with him.
I caught up with him, I caught up with him,
I caught up with him, I caught up with him.
Beneath the Two Setting, I caught up with him.
(Yellow Coyote) With the Yellow Prayerstick in his hand....
(continued as in first stanza)

Beneath Where the Stars Turn, I caught up with him.
(Black Coyote) With the Black Prayerstick in his hand....
(continues as in second stanza)

This song is repeated three times in the same manner as Song 89—beginning with south, then with west, and finally with north.

92. Song, Sixth Evening

He gives the Prayerstick to me, he gives the Prayerstick to me,
He gives the Prayerstick to me, he gives the Prayerstick to me.
Beneath the Two Rising, he gives the Prayerstick to me.
White Coyote, White Prayerstick in hand,
he gives the Prayerstick to me.
Happiness before me, he gives the Prayerstick to me.

Happiness behind me, he gives the Prayerstick to me.
He gives the Prayerstick to me, he gives the Prayerstick to me,
He gives the Prayerstick to me, he gives the Prayerstick to me.
Beneath the Two Above, he gives the Prayerstick to me.
Blue Coyote, Blue Prayerstick in hand,
he gives the Prayerstick to me.
Happiness behind me, he gives the Prayerstick to me.
Happiness before me, he gives the Prayerstick to me.
He gives the Prayerstick to me, he gives the Prayerstick to me,
He gives the Prayerstick to me, he gives the Prayerstick to me.
Beneath the Two Setting, he gives the Prayerstick to me.
Yellow Coyote, Yellow Prayerstick in hand....
(continued as in first stanza)

Beneath Where the Stars Turn, he gives the Prayerstick to me.
Black Coyote, Black Prayerstick in hand....
(continued as in second stanza)

This song is repeated three times in the same manner as Song 89—beginning with south, then with west, and finally with north.

93. Song, Sixth Evening

He came back with me, he came back with me,
He came back with me, he came back with me.
From Beneath the Two Rising, he came back with me.
The White Coyote, he came back with me.
With Happiness before me, he came back with me.
With Happiness behind me, he came back with me.
He came back with me, he came back with me,
He came back with me, he came back with me.
From Beneath the Two Above....
(continued with "Blue Coyote" and "Happiness behind")

From Beneath the Two Setting....
(continued with "Yellow Coyote" and "Happiness before")

From Beneath Where the Stars Turn....
(continued with "Black Coyote" and "Happiness behind")

This song is repeated three times in the same manner as Song 89—beginning with south, then with west, and finally with north.

94. Song, Sixth Evening

They are now sitting by me, they are now sitting by me,
They are now sitting by me, they are now sitting by me.

From Beneath the Two Rising, they are now sitting by me.
The White Coyote People, they are now sitting by me.
With Happiness before me, they are now sitting by me.
With Happiness behind me, they are now sitting by me.
  They are now sitting by me, they are now sitting by me,
  They are now sitting by me, they are now sitting by me.
From Beneath the Two Above....
(continued with "Blue Coyote" and "Happiness behind")

From Beneath the Two Setting....
(continued with "Yellow Coyote" and "Happiness before")

From Beneath Where the Stars Turn....
(continued with "Black Coyote" and "Happiness behind")

This song is repeated three times in the same manner as Song 89—beginning with south, then with west, and finally with north.

SEVENTH EVENING

The following basket-drum songs are chanted in unison on the seventh evening of the Coyoteway ceremonial:

98. Song, Seventh Evening

  This is the Hogan, this is the Hogan,
  This is the Hogan, this is the Hogan.
This is the Hogan given to me....
(This song is the same as Song 72.)

99. Song, Seventh Evening

The One walking in the fields, the Boy, is found.
Beneath the Two Rising, he is found.
Over the White Mountain, he is found.
With White Corn around him, he is found.
Over the Path of Cornpollen, he is found.
Over Morning Twilight, he is found.
With Round Corn around him, he is found.
  He is my Relative, he is found.
  He is my Relative, he is found.
  He is my Relative, he is found.
  He is my Relative, he is found.
The One walking in the fields, the Girl, is found.
Beneath the Two Setting, she is found.
Over the Yellow Mountain, she is found.
With Yellow Corn around her, she is found.

Over the Path of Cornpollen, she is found.
Over Evening Twilight, she is found.
With Round Corn around her, she is found.
   She is my Relative, she is found.
   She is my Relative, she is found.
   She is my Relative, she is found.
   She is my Relative, she is found.
The One walking in the fields, the Boy, is found.
Beneath the Two Above, he is found.
Over the Blue Mountain, he is found.
With Blue Corn around him, he is found.
Over the Path of Cornpollen, he is found.
Over the Roots of Sunlight, he is found.
With Round Corn around him, he is found.
   He is my Relative, he is found.
   He is my Relative, he is found.
   He is my Relative, he is found.
   He is my Relative, he is found.
The One walking in the fields, the Girl, is found.
Beneath Where the Stars Turn, she is found.
Over Black Mountain, she is found.
With Black Corn around her, she is found.
Over the Path of Cornpollen, she is found.
Over the Roots of Rain, she is found.
With Round Corn around her, she is found.
   She is my Relative, she is found.
   She is my Relative, she is found.
   She is my Relative, she is found.
   She is my Relative, she is found.
   This is the Hogan, this is the Hogan,
   This is the Hogan, this is the Hogan.

This song is chanted four times in the same directional sequence.
The Boys in the east and south, and the Girls in the west and north, are
Coyotes.

100. Song, Seventh Evening

   From far away, he comes out.
   From far away, he comes out.
   From far away, he comes out.
   From far away, he comes out.
From under the Two Rising, he comes out.
From the Hogan, in white fur, he comes out.

Far away from this Hogan, he comes out.
With Happiness before him, he comes out.
With Happiness behind him, he comes out.
  From far away, he comes out.
  From far away, he comes out.
  From far away, he comes out.
  From far away, he comes out.
From under the Two Setting, he comes out.
From the Hogan, in yellow fur, he comes out.
Far away from this Hogan, he comes out.
With Happiness behind him, he comes out.
With Happiness before him, he comes out.
  From far away, he comes out.
  From far away, he comes out.
  From far away, he comes out.
  From far away, he comes out.
From under the Two Above, he comes out.
From the Hogan, in blue fur, he comes out....
(continued as in first stanza)

From beneath Where the Stars Turn, he comes out.
From the Hogan, in the black fur, he comes out....
(continued as in second stanza)

This song is chanted four times in the same directional sequence. The phrases "in white fur—or yellow, blue, and black fur" are ambiguous. They may define the emerging Coyote-persons, the hogans from where they emerge, or both.

EIGHTH EVENING

The following basket-drum songs are chanted in unison on the eighth evening of the Coyoteway ceremonial:

104. Song, Eighth Evening

With my Mind I walk in the presence of the Sun,[2]
with my Mind I walk, with my Mind I walk,
with my Mind I walk, with my Mind I walk.
Beneath the Two Rising, with my Mind I walk.
Where White Coyote Medicine is, with my Mind I walk.
Where White Air is, with my Mind I walk.

---

[2]"With my Mind I walk," or, "In proximity of my Mind (Consciousness) I walk." The mind of the patient is here regarded as an independent personage.

On the Path of yellow Cornpollen, with my Mind I walk.
Among Rainbows, with my Mind I walk.
Amid round Corn, with my Mind I walk, with my Mind I walk.

Beneath the Two Setting, with my Mind I walk.
Where Yellow Coyote Medicine is, with my Mind I walk.
Where Yellow Air is, with my Mind I walk.
On the Path of yellow Cornpollen, with my Mind I walk.
In Sunshine, with my Mind I walk.
Amid round Corn, with my Mind I walk, with my Mind I walk.

Beneath the Two Above, with my Mind I walk.
Where Blue Coyote Medicine is, with my Mind I walk.
Where Blue Air is, with my Mind I walk.
On the Path of yellow Cornpollen, with my Mind I walk.
In Sunshine, with my Mind I walk.
Amid round Corn, with my Mind I walk, with my Mind I walk.

Beneath Where the Stars Turn, with my Mind I walk.
Where Black Coyote Medicine is, with my Mind I walk.
In the Black Mountains, with my Mind I walk.
On the Path of yellow Cornpollen, with my Mind I walk.
Among the Roots (Streaks) of Rain, with my Mind I walk.
Amid round Corn, with my Mind I walk, with my Mind I walk.
  With my Mind I walk in the presence of the Sun,
  with my Mind I walk, with my Mind I walk,
  with my Mind I walk, with my Mind I walk.

105. Song, Eighth Evening

I am looking for my Mind in the presence of the Sun,[3]
I am looking for my Mind, I am looking for my Mind,
I am looking for my Mind, I am looking for my Mind.
Beneath the Two Rising, I am looking for my Mind....
(continued after the pattern of Song 104)

106. Song, Eighth Evening

I have found my Mind in the presence of the Sun,[4]
I have found my Mind, I have found my Mind,
I have found my Mind, I have found my Mind.
Beneath the Two Rising, I have found my Mind....
(continued after the pattern of Song 104)

---

[3]"I am looking for my Mind," or, "I am struggling for Consciousness."

[4]"I have found my Mind," or, "I am beginning to perceive."

107. Song, Eighth Evening

I am bringing back my Mind in the presence of the Sun,[5]
I am bringing back my Mind, I am bringing back my Mind,
I am bringing back my Mind, I am bringing back my Mind.
Beneath the Two Rising, I am bringing back my Mind....
(continued after the pattern of Song 104)

108. Song, Eighth Evening

I am reviving my Mind in the presence of the Sun,[6]
I am reviving my Mind, I am reviving my Mind,
I am reviving my Mind, I am reviving my Mind.
Beneath the Two Rising, I am reviving my Mind....
(continued after the pattern of Song 104)

109. Song, Eighth Evening

Now my Mind is walking with me in the presence of the Sun,[7]
now my Mind is walking with me,
now my Mind is walking with me,
now my Mind is walking with me,
now my Mind is walking with me.
Beneath the Two Rising, now my Mind is walking with me....
(continued after the pattern of Song 104)

110. Song, Eighth Evening

Now my Mind is remade for me in the presence of the Sun,[8]
now my Mind is remade for me, now my Mind is remade for me,
now my Mind is remade for me, now my Mind is remade for me.
Beneath the Two Rising, now my Mind is remade for me....
(continued after the pattern of Song 104)

111. Song, Eighth Evening

Now my Mind returns with me in the presence of the Sun,[9]
now my Mind returns with me, now my Mind returns with me,
now my Mind returns with me, now my Mind returns with me.
Beneath the Two Rising, now my Mind returns with me....
(continued after the pattern of Song 104)

---

[5]"I am bringing back my Mind," or, "I am regaining Consciousness."

[6]"I am reviving my Mind"—as one would teach a baby to walk.

[7]"Now my Mind is walking with me"—it has learned to go on its own power.

[8]"Now my Mind is remade for me," or, "we are together again."

[9]"Now my Mind returns with me," or, "now I am starting back with my Mind, side by side." Mind and body function together.

112. Song, Eighth Evening

Now I am sitting with my Mind in the presence of the Sun,[10]
now I am sitting with my Mind, now I am sitting with my Mind,
now I am sitting with my Mind, now I am sitting with my Mind.
Beneath the Two Rising, now I am sitting with my Mind....
(continued after the pattern of Song 104)

113. Song, Eighth Evening

With Black Bead as my feet, with this I walk.
Clothed in Black Coyote, with this I walk.
Clothed in Black Water, with this I walk.
Clothed in Arrows, with this I walk.
He (Coyote) is hiding behind me, with him I walk.
He is hiding before me, with him I walk.
   With these, with these, everything is made Happiness.
   With these, with these, everything is made Happiness.
   With these everything is made Happiness.
   With these everything is made Happiness.
   With these, Happiness behind me.
   With these, Happiness before me.
   With these, with these, everything is made Happiness.
   With these, with these, everything is made Happiness.
With Turquoise as my feet, with this I walk.
Clothed in Blue Coyote, with this I walk.
In the Place of Rainbow, there I walk.
In Rain behind the Rainbow, there I walk.
Among ripe Plants behind the Rain, there I walk.
With Roots of Sunshine, with these I walk.
Healing Power behind these, with this I walk.
   With these, with these, everything is made Happiness....
(continued as in first stanza)

114. Song, Eighth Evening

They are singing for me, they are singing for me,
They are singing for me, they are singing for me.
The Talking-god's Son I am, they are singing for me.
Where White Bead points down, they are singing for me.
Clothed in Black Air, they are singing for me.
Surrounded by Black Lightning, they are singing for me.

---

[10]"Now I am sitting with my mind"—side by side in the hogan. Consciousness and well-being are present as the patient sits in the hogan.

With Happiness before me, they are singing for me.
Traveling on the Roots of Morning Dawn, they are singing for me.
    With these, with these, everything is made Happiness....
(same refrain as in Song 113)

The Calling-god's Son I am, they are singing for me.
Where the Turquoise points down, they are singing for me.
Clothed in Blue Corn-ripener Beetles, they are singing for me.
In the Place of Rainbow, they are singing for me.
In Rain behind the Rainbow, they are singing for me.
Among ripe Plants behind the Rain, they are singing for me.
At the Roots of Sunshine, with these I walk.
Healing Power behind these, with this I walk.
    With these, with these, everything is made Happiness....
(same refrain as in Song 113)

115. Song, Eighth Evening

    It is raining on me, it is raining on me,
    It is raining on me, it is raining on me.
The Talking-god's Son I am, it is raining on me.
With White Bead as my shoes, it is raining on us.
Where White Bead points down, it is raining on us.
Clothed in Black Corn-ripener Beetles, it is raining on us.
Clothed in Black Water, it is raining on us.
Clothed in Black Cloud, it is raining on us.
In the Place of Rainbow, it is raining on us.
In Rain behind the Rainbow, it is raining on us.
Among ripe Plants behind the Rain, it is raining on us.
At the Roots of Morning Dawn, it is raining on us.
    With these, with these, everything is made Happiness....
(same refrain as in Song 113)

The Calling-god's Son I am, it is raining on me.
Where the Turquoise points down, it is raining on us.
Clothed in the Blue Prayerstick, it is raining on us.
Clothed in Blue Sky, it is raining on us.
In the Place of Rainbow, it is raining on us.
In Rain behind the Rainbow, it is raining on us.
Among ripe Plants behind the Rain, it is raining on us.
At the Roots of Sunshine, it is raining on us.
Healing Power behind these, it is raining on us.
    With these, with these, everything is made Happiness....
(same refrain as in Song 113)

116. Song, Eighth Evening

The blessing is given, the blessing is given,
The blessing is given, the blessing is given.
The Talking-god's Son I am, the blessing is given.
Where White Bead points down, the blessing is given.
Clothed in the Black Prayerstick, the blessing is given.
Clothed in Black Cloud, the blessing is given.
In the Place of Rainbow, the blessing is given.
In the Place of Ripened Plants, the blessing is given.
In the Place of Rain, the blessing is given.
At the Roots of Morning Dawn, the blessing is given.
With Rain behind me, the blessing is given.
With Healing Power before the Rain, the blessing is given.
　　With these, with these, everything is made Happiness....
(same refrain as in Song 113)

The Calling-god's Son I am, the blessing is given.
Where Turquoise points down, the blessing is given.
Clothed in Blue Cornripener Beetles, the blessing is given.
Clothed in the Black Prayerstick, the blessing is given.
With Rain behind me, the blessing is given.
Among ripe Plants behind the Rain, the blessing is given.
At the Roots of Sunshine, the blessing is given.
With Healing Power following these, the blessing is given.
　　With these, with these, everything is made Happiness....
(same refrain as in Song 113)

BURNING THE FEATHERS

Each session of basket-drum singing ends with a Feather-burning Rite—the same procedure which earlier has been described in connection with the Unraveling and the Fire Ceremonies. As was the case then, a feather mixture is sprinkled on a hot coal, the smoke is fanned and rubbed on the patient, then the coal is quenched with water. The extinguished coal, which has absorbed many of the patient's troubles, is carried away while he is temporarily outside. When the patient returns he sits again at his regular place. The priestly singer sprinkles cornmeal in the four directions and explains in a subdued voice that the act of burning and removing the feathers is not sufficient by itself. The positive blessings of sacred meal, power of life, must be added to heal the wounds left behind by the exorcised feathery witchcraft arrows.

After each ceremony follows a period of rest. Whoever feels so inclined, is free to play a game of cards.

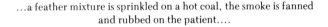

...a feather mixture is sprinkled on a hot coal, the smoke is fanned
and rubbed on the patient....

...then the coal is quenched with water.

After each ceremony follows a period of rest. Whoever feels so inclined is free to play a game of cards.

Sandpainting Ceremonies

The Problem of Naming the Yé'ii

The Navajo language has three names to refer to the gods—*yé'ii*, *hashch'ééh*, *diné dighinii*. In usage these names overlap quite easily. Some *yé'ii* are *hashch'ééh*, and some *hashch'ééh* are *diné dighinii* (Holy People). The name *yé'ii* is mostly reserved for those gods who appear in ceremonials in the form of masked human impersonators.

On the fifth, sixth, and seventh mornings of the Coyoteway ceremonial, during the sandpainting ceremonies, a masked *yé'ii*-impersonator appears. What is the name of the god whom he impersonates? This question is directly linked to the identity of three other *yé'ii* figures who appear on the eighth morning. The second figure of this group is identical with the single *yé'ii* of the three preceding days. Our discussion may therefore focus on the identities of the entire triad.

The name of the first *yé'ii* figure on that culminating eighth morning is beyond doubt. He is the *yé'iibicheii*, grandfather and leader of all the Navajo gods. As an authentic hunter deity he wears a buckskin over his shoulders and carries a fawnskin pouch; in the middle of his face, however, is painted the mark of Pueblo Indian influence— a maize plant. Impersonated by a man, he appears on the eighth morning to bless the patient, the other *yé'ii*-impersonators, and the sandpainting. As an outward symbol of his blessings he sprinkles pollen.

The second *yé'ii* in our Coyoteway ceremonial is also impersonated by a man. His blue mask and his apparel are identical with those of the *yé'ii* figure of the preceding three sandpainting ceremonies. When he appears together with the other two gods on the eighth day, his actions match those of the preceding days—despite the fact that on the last day, in our ceremonial, a different man played the role. The only added function on the eighth day involves his carrying a stuffed Blue Coyote (gray fox). His overall appearance and costume correspond to those of the anthropomorphic lead figures in the sandpainting of the same day.

The third *yé'ii* is impersonated by a woman. She wears a blue mask, identical to that of the second *yé'ii*. While her male counterpart carries a stuffed Coyote, she carries a basket containing ears of maize, with eagle tail feathers radiating from it. The same basket can be found depicted in the hands of all the anthropomorphic follower-*yé'ii* in the sandpainting of the eighth day. Both the second and the third *yé'ii*-impersonators are thus, via stuffed animal and basket, clearly identical with the *yé'ii* figures in the fourth sandpainting. On this point all the participants agree.

Of the two blue-masked figures the third in the triad is easiest to name. All our participants, and all the written sources, agree that she is *hashch'ééh bi'áád*, the Female God. Luke Cook identified her more precisely as a daughter of the Talking-god. Man With Palomino Horse referred to her as Talking-god's Female.

This leaves only the problem concerning the identity of the second *yé'ii*-impersonator. And here we must divide the information we have with regard to specific informants and sources. Luke Cook, who interpreted all *yé'ii* figures in the sandpaintings as anthropomorphic Coyote People, consistently identified the second *yé'ii*-impersonator with Coyote-carrying Coyotes in the underworld. The blue mask, and the stuffed "blue fox" in his hands, links this deity with the south. Accordingly, the second *yé'ii* is Blue Coyote from the underworld's south. On three successive days he appears in the microcosm of the sandpainting without his animal manifestation. On the last day he is depicted in the sandpainting in both his human and his animal forms. He appears impersonated, each day exactly as the sandpainters have portrayed and invited him in their sandpainting. If this interpretation is carried to its logical conclusion, then the third *yé'ii*-impersonator is not merely a Female God, but Blue Coyote Woman from the underworld's south.

However, Man With Palomino Horse understands his work a little differently. The *yé'ii* figures in the sandpaintings represent simply anthropomorphic gods—not necessarily anthropomorphic Coyote People. The god-impersonators who appear in the sandpainting ceremonies are simply *yé'ii*, nothing more. The second figure in the triad just happens to be the *yé'ii* who carries Coyote. He is a god who by way of the stuffed gray fox "makes use of" Coyote as one would make use of a tool. In answer to my direct question about the gender of the second and third impersonators, our Coyoteway singer produced some rather puzzling news: both are Female Gods. I am convinced that every reader who examines the photographic evidence will agree with me that the second *yé'ii* is impersonated by a male. Seeing my disbelief clearly written on my face, the singer struggled for a more congenial answer: the first is the Talking-god, the second is the Calling-god, and the third is the Female God. This made sense. A blue-masked *yé'ii* belongs to the south, and Calling-god is indeed the best candidate for claiming this mask. Talking-god and Calling-god frequently appear together. All seems to be well with this last emphatic explanation by the practitioner—except that the known masks of Calling-god in the Navajo repertoire do not match the mask of our second *yé'ii*. If the masks which are used in the most elaborate "*yé'iibicheii* ceremonial," the Night Chant, can be used for comparison, then the mask of our second impersonator is indeed that of a female deity.

It is doubtful whether our Coyoteway singer will ever be able to come forth with more definite explanations. His *yé'ii* figures, whether male or female, have no precise counterparts in the Coyoteway myth as he knows it. Rather, it seems that for him the *yé'ii*-impersonations are additions to the ceremonial procedures; also, it seems that they are dictated more by tradition or by competition with other "*yé'iibicheii*" ceremonials than by rational necessity. Moreover, his reduction of the animal manifestations of Coyote to the level of tools is in disagreement with the Coyote mysticism expressed throughout the ceremonial in rituals and songs. It appears that our priest has projected into his present answers his own latent ambitions for taking control. To some extent, by performing Coyoteway, he himself has begun using Coyote as a tool. This portrait of the singer may well be exaggerated. Nevertheless, his patient, who was about to be initiated as a novice, still experienced the presence of Coyote mystically, after the manner of shamanic possession by some greater-than-human divine being. Luke Cook has been participating in Coyoteway ceremonials too long for having his understanding of them taken lightly.

By surveying the literary sources one gets the impression that perhaps in Coyoteway, at least since the time when it was being performed with sandpaintings and with *yé'ii*-impersonators, the ambiguity about its divine actors has always been present. Father Berard Haile (1947, p. 39) voiced the same complaint even with regard to the better known *yé'ii* figures of the Nightway ceremonial. Thus, if we should ask our Coyoteway singer again whether the second impersonator always wore the same type of mask, we can easily predict his answer. Whether he knows better or not, he would have to answer yes. As long as he performs the ceremonial he will have to claim that everything he does is true to tradition and to the original instructions of the gods.

Before leaving the identity of the first *yé'ii* for the reader to decide, we must consult the written sources. They are scarce indeed. In 1910 the Franciscan Fathers wrote in their *Ethnologic Dictionary* (p. 392): "In the Coyote dance, which is now extinct, three personators of Talking-god, the Fringed Mouth, and a Female God appeared. It is said that the Fringed Mouth danced carrying a live kit-fox in his hands. This was done inside the hogan." Father Berard Haile (1947, p. 65) tells us that in the Nightway ceremonial the Fringed Mouth is named after "a fluff of blue fox" which encircles his mouth.

In the same report Father Berard also identifies the *yé'ii*-persons of the Coyoteway ceremonial (p. 77): On the last day of the ceremonial three *yé'ii* appear, Talking-god and two Female Gods. "One of the female *yé'ii* carries a *mą'ii*—blue fox—which is prepared with care so that it resembles a live one. This he applies to the patient to sanctify him. The other (female) *yé'ii* carries a basket with cornmeal which he applies to the patient as in Nightway. In Nightway he (this female *yé'ii*) carries a white and yellow ear of corn which he applies to the patient. According to its legend the three *yé'ii* (Talking-god and two Female Gods) appeared at the Coyoteway ceremonial. Hence singers of this chantway own these masks and do not borrow them from Nightway." *Tséyi'nii* (1934), in the second Coyoteway myth reprinted (Chapter 10, paragraph 4), also mentions two Female Gods in connection with the Talking-god.

Then, Mary Wheelwright, in 1931, obtained a Coyoteway myth from *yoo' hataałii* who had learned it from *hastiin neez* (reprinted in Chapter 9). From this version we learn that "on the last night the patient stands on a buckskin holding ground meal in a basket and three gods, Talking-god, Coyote, and Female God come to the patient and Female God holds a shell with cornpollen in it and four eagle tail feathers radiating from the center." This last portion of information is the more interesting if we consider that our Man With Palomino Horse derives the sandpainting portion of his ceremonial— thus presumably also matters pertaining to *yé'ii*-impersonations—from *hastiin neez* also.

Thus, according to our available data, our second *yé'ii* can be as many as five different kinds of divine beings: Fringed Mouth, a second Female God, Coyote, a Female Coyote, or Calling-god. Knowing the context in which the name of Calling-god was given, I discount this possibility from the outset.

Fringed Mouth is a candidate for very early versions of Coyote-way, especially because the fluff which is present around his mouth comes from the "blue fox." While this association of the Coyote Carrier with the stuffed gray fox could have brought Fringed Mouth into the Coyoteway ceremonial at an early date, another line of explanation appears at least plausible. On the ninth night of each Nightway cere-monial "Talking-god, Fringed Mouth, and Humpback, approach the hogan. The patient goes outside to face them and here Fringed Mouth motions over him from all sides and accompanies these motions with his call… (this) may be considered the finale of 'sanctification' cere-monies of Nightway" (Haile 1947, p. 72). A similar such triad of *yé'ii*-impersonators may have been adopted by Coyoteway singers at a very early date, but the reference by the Franciscan Fathers to Fringed Mouth as the second *yé'ii* in Coyoteway can also rest on a limited functional parallel. The Coyote Carrier in the finale of Coyoteway functions in a similar manner as Fringed Mouth in the finale of Nightway. For interpreting the version of Coyoteway which we have here at hand, the participation of Fringed Mouth can not be assumed. No informant now living mentions him.

We must puzzle now over the first claim of Man With Palomino Horse, that both our second and third impersonators represent Female Gods. This claim is supported from three directions. In the first place, the mask of the second is identical with the mask of the third. Secondly, Father Berard as quoted above, and assumedly from a reliable source, tells us that Coyoteway calls for a Talking-god and two Female God impersonations. Thirdly, *tséyi'nii* in his myth, given in Chapter 10, paragraph 4, mentions two Female Gods together with the Talking-god.

But, if this is true, why are not both Female Gods impersonated by women? The answer to this question, too, is illuminated by looking to Nightway practice for precedents. Washington Matthews (1902, p. 17f) reported the occasional presence of up to six different Female God impersonators in Nightway. In most cases the goddesses are impersonated by a boy or a man of low stature. He wears an ornate skirt around the hips and a belt ornamented with silver from which a fox skin dangles behind. All this matches our second figure in Coyote-way very well. Washington Matthews continues with saying, that on the last night of Nightway the character of Female God is sometimes assumed by women. The female impersonators are fully clothed in Navajo woman's dress. That Nightway practice can be taken as proto-type for the Coyoteway *yé'ii*-impersonations is suggested already by a fact mentioned earlier in the Haile quotation (1947, p. 77)—the ears of maize in the basket of our third impersonator in Coyoteway are a recent borrowing from Nightway. Sufficient information is thus available to accept our singer's first answer: The second and third impersonations in our ceremonial are both Female Gods.

Now only the most difficult question remains to be asked. If both are Female Gods, to what species of beings do they belong? Are they anthropomorphic gods? Are they goddesses of the hunt after the fashion of *hashch'ééh oołt'oh* in Nightway? Or are they intended to represent Female Coyotes? Navajo gods still today participate in the mythological stratum of prehuman flux—they are not restricted to certain anthropomorphic, theriomorphic, or occupational manifestations; they can equally well hide and show themselves in the shimmering lights of dawn, midday, and sunset; total invisibility is also in their power. Nevertheless, in a Coyoteway healing ceremonial, where for nine nights the songs of Coyote People are chanted, the most likely female deities present—it would seem—could be Coyotes.

Whatever degree of uncertainty about the identities of the *yé'ii* characters in our ceremonial the singer communicated to me, it is outweighed by the impressions which he left on his apprentice. Luke Cook knew that all, impersonators and sandpainting figures in our ceremonial—apart from the Talking-god—are Coyotes. This state of affairs bestows full credence on some data which elsewhere has been obtained from a certain "Big Mustache." Big Mustache is the same as Many Whiskers, the man whom our practitioner has identified as his grandfather and teacher. In 1929 this old Coyoteway singer gave to Laura Armer the same sandpaintings which our singer received from *hastiin neez*. Better yet, he identified all his sandpainting figures as Coyote Girls. (See Chapter 12—Sandpainting Reproductions, Sandpaintings 2 through 5 by Big Mustache.)

The presence of female masks in the Coyoteway ceremonial is quite reasonable if credence is given to an episode in the *yoo' hataałii* and *hastiin neez* version of the myth reprinted in Chapter 9. The first Coyoteway singer who ventured into the underworld has married two Coyote Girls from each of the four directions—exactly the number of *yé'ii* needed for the sandpaintings. Marriage, in this context, signifies a mystic union between a shaman and the divine Coyote People from whom he receives his powers. Marriage implies that the partners are members of the same species. Judged by their color, our blue-masked and white-painted female Coyotes belong either to the blue south or to the white east. Our second and third *yé'ii*-impersonators are Coyote Girls either from the underworld's east or south!

This place in the book is suited as well as any for briefly summarizing Coyoteway theology. How many Coyote gods are there? The answer to this question depends on the context in which the question is asked.

While Fire Ceremonies are in progress, the singer recognizes twelve Coyote People; twelve are contacted by way of prayersticks and prayers: four "Shouting Coyotes," four Coyotes simply identified by their directional colors, together with Hidden Boy, White Dawn Girl, Flint Hill Boy, and Water Girl.

Later references, in songs, to the Adulterous Coyote and the Staggering Coyote seem to have no specific connection with any of the twelve. These names appear to be designations of Coyote in general. Many morality stories about these Coyotes are being told today among the Navajo. What our practitioner emphasized repeatedly, however, is that he is dealing with the same Coyote. The answer here is that there is only one Coyote. This assertion is supported by inclusion of his song about the sliding lizards (Song 74)—an episode usually attributed to the staggering or trotting Coyote.

There is still another way of looking at Coyote People numerically. At a meeting when we discussed with our Coyoteway singer the cause and remedy of Coyote illness, he flatly pronounced that there are alto-gether two Coyotes. The bad Coyote causes illness, the good Coyote heals. A similar dualism is delineated by *tséyi'nii* in Chapter 10, para-graphs 3 and 4: bad Coyote People from the lower world cause illness; the good Coyote People down there provided the Coyoteway healing ceremonial. There is a slight hint in the ceremonial that Adulterous Coyote is the same as the Bad One. In Songs 78 and 79 the fact is celebrated that "the song he sings does not affect me." But then, immediately in Song 80 the same Adulterous Coyote "makes the Medicine." Considering the debate in my own Hebrew-Christian tradition, about whether the almighty God causes only good things to happen or whether he is also responsible for what has come to be attributed to the Devil, I felt that I should not burden Man With Palomino Horse with redundant questions. Faced with the presence overpowering evil, every kind of theist is sooner or later tempted, by the easy solution of an ethical dualism, to subtract something from the scope of his one god.

Coyoteway theology is made easier if we return to the simplified world of the sandpainting. Not twelve Coyotes, or two or one, but eight Coyote Girls are present and accounted for. The bad Coyote is not mentioned at all in that context—unless one should count here the appearance of a Coyote Witch-person in *tséyi'nii*'s Coyoteway myth (Chapter 10, paragraph 3). The objective of the ceremony is to obtain health and power to heal. For this purpose the eight Coyote Girls, who through marriage empowered the first Coyoteway shaman, are sufficient. If additional blessings are needed in the ceremonial from outside the jurisdiction of the Coyote People, the Talking-god, grandfather and chief of the Navajo pantheon, guarantees these with his bodily appearance on the eighth morning. The occasional references in prayer and songs to Calling-god present the latter as a helper, or possibly as an extension, of the Talking-god.

Significant is the form and appearance of the Coyote People in the underworld. They are anthropomorphic beings who dress themselves in Coyote skins only when they are leaving their homes. I have explained the nature of traditional hunter gods in relation to "prehuman flux" (Luckert 1975). In the beginning all "people" were able to exchange their appearances like clothes. When eventually mankind and many animals became fixed permanently in their present shapes, the gods remained in a state of prehuman flux. It was therefore not necessary for the first Coyoteway shaman to learn his ceremonial from animal-shaped Coyote manifestations; he learned it from their anthropomorphic and divine prototypes in the underworld. Anthropomorphs can talk. As manifestations of *logos* they are quite capable of revealing their powerful songs and rational instructions for the ceremonial. It is this same universal human search for the divine *logos* by which also the white Talking-god of the east has been discovered as the chief of the Navajo pantheon. The logic of this development is clear: if the substratum of human existence is not personal or anthropomorphically intelligible, then what is man?

In structure and form Coyoteway differs from Nightway and other ceremonials at some points. Leland Wyman has informed me that in chantways which he has attended the sweat-emetic rite has always preceded the offering rite. He also explained that three additional ritual procedures are standard parts in most other five and nine-night ceremonials; these are (1) the consecration of the hogan on the first night before unraveling by applying cornmeal on the roof beams and by putting oak twigs in the rafters in the four cardinal directions; (2) setting out plumed wands on a little mound east of the hogan before dawn on days when sandpaintings are made; and (3) figure painting and token tying on the last day before the sandpainting rite.

The first of these procedures, I must admit, could possibly have been overlooked by me while I was getting my gear ready—though I doubt this. Then, branches from various bushes, including yucca leaves for the drumstick, were indeed stored in the rafters by the door beginning with noontime after the rites on the third morning. No special purpose was ascribed to this aside from storing and unthawing for later gear making. The second of these "standard procedures" was perhaps omitted in our ceremonial because of the deep snow and the blizzard conditions which prevailed outside. The third of these procedures could have been performed on the last day inside the hogan while I was recording from the outside. This seems very unlikely, though, because the patient has told us repeatedly what went on inside and what he remembered to have been the complete ritual sequence.

That the present nine-night Coyoteway sequence and performance is a kind of modified adaptation from Nightway seems to have emerged clearly from the foregoing discussions. But since Nightway performances themselves seem to be capable of varying with regard to the identity of god-impersonators from one to the next, it should come as no surprise when Matthews and Tozzer (Tozzer 1909, pp. 314-16) have also reported two different Nightway sequences. Since presently we do not have enough historical information about these and other variations, it would be premature to speculate about whether, at a given point in time and place, a Coyoteway shaman has been induced to visit the underworld under the tutelage of a certain Nightway practitioner.

The One-yé'ii Ceremony

THE SANDPAINTINGS

In a Navajo sandpainting nothing is actually painted; instead, colored sands and powders are trickled from between the fingers on a smooth patch of ordinary brown sand.

In the afternoon, before our first sandpainting is to be made, Luke Cook, his youngest son, and I, drive to an outcropping of varicolored sandstone, about five miles of smooth snow from the ceremonial hogan. Pieces of different color are chipped from the boulders. Then back home, red, yellow, and white powders are obtained by grinding rocks of these colors. Black is made of charcoal. A grayish "blue" is obtained by mixing white with black.

Sandpaintings are made on the fifth, sixth, seventh, and eighth mornings of the Coyoteway ceremonial. The first three sandpaintings are prepared for the lone appearance of Blue Coyote Girl. The fourth sandpainting, on the eighth morning, is made in preparation for the visit of the yé'iibicheii (the Talking-god) and two Coyote Girls.

Shortly before sunrise the fireplace is moved to one side. Ordinarily it would be taken outside, but freezing weather and heavy snowstorms keep coming at regular intervals throughout the nine days. Without any heat at all the fingers of the sandpainters would stiffen and so become unable to trickle the required fine lines and even patches of colored sands.

A large patch of sand is leveled at the center of the hogan. Directly below the smokehole a bowl is inserted and filled with water. This bowl represents the hole of emergence at the center of the world. According to Pueblo-influenced Navajo mythology, the human race emerged there at the beginning of time; the water in the bowl suggests the flood which after the emergence has threatened to overtake the people.[1] This hole of emergence, placed at the center of the hogan, becomes the center of the mini-world or microcosm which is about to be constructed around it.

Healing in the great expanse of the wide world is extremely difficult. Not even the most able practitioner would claim that he can oversee and respond to all possible situations and power configurations in the entire world. A controlable environment, a sandpainted microcosm, is therefore constructed. The world is reduced symbolically to the presences of the most essential agents of power for the purpose at hand. The range of possible situations and contingencies can so be overseen and can, to some measure, be even controlled. To understand this nearly scientific procedure it must be understood, however, that symbolic representations in traditional Navajo thought participate with their essences in the subject matter which they represent. Symbolic representations are always extensions of a greater reality.

The production of a sandpainting should perhaps be defined as a "folk-art." All participants help in producing it. The practitioner decides and supervises the structure of the design by constantly appealing to tradition and to sketches which he produces from his satchel. He himself covers the water-filled bowl, or hole of emergence, with *kétłoh* powder, the rub-on medicine which has been used since the first Unraveling ceremony. Charcoal powder is sprinkled on top of this. Then the entire spot of hidden moisture is circled, first with white, then with yellow and black rims.

Using a straightedge, a sandpainter then produces a white-framed red-and-blue rainbow to the west, south, and east of the hole of emergence. A corresponding black-and-white pattern north of the center is made to represent sunrays or "roots of sunlight." Utmost concentration is required for producing uniform designs and lines.

Then, corresponding to the four directions, white *yé'ii* figures—Coyote Girls—are painted in the east. Blue Ones are painted in the south, Yellow Ones in the west, and Black Ones in the north. The color of their bodies identifies their directional associations. All the while the singer supervises and rarely touches the colored sands himself. Instead,

---

[1]For more information on this subject, see Karl W. Luckert, *Olmec Religion*, University of Oklahoma Press, 1976.

Luke Cook, his youngest son, and I drive to an outcropping of varicolored sandstone, about five miles of smooth snow from the ceremonial hogan.

Pieces of different colors are chipped from the boulders.

Using a straightedge, a sandpainter then produces a white-framed
red-and-blue rainbow to the west... of the hole of emergence.

Utmost concentration is required for producing uniform designs and lines.

he repaints the masks which will be used later by the *yé'ii*-impersonators.

The most important features in the reduced symbolic world of the Coyoteway ceremonial are the central Hole of Emergence, the sacred *yé'ii*-People situated symmetrically among Plants of Maize, and Rainbows who define the boundary of the whole and surround the center of the world. The hole of emergence, in this context, facilitates the reoccurence of two important mythical events—the general origin of healthy human beings in the surface world, and the institution of the Coyoteway ceremonial subsequent to the general emergence. Coyoteway originates with the Coyote People in the underworld, anew, in every healing or initiation performance.

All the while the singer supervises and rarely touches
the colored sands himself.

Instead, he repaints the masks which will be
used later by the *yé'ii*-impersonators.

The shamanic hero, that is, the first human to learn the Coyote-way ceremonial, journeyed into the underworld and found there the four kinds of Coyote People. He visited White Coyotes to the east, Blue Coyotes to the south, Yellow Ones to the west, and Black Ones to the north of the underworld's center. Coyote power was transmitted to the shamanic hero by a process of marriage—he became one of the Coyote People. He married two girls from among each of the four types of Coyote People. It would be difficult to do anything more thoroughly or to accomplish something more completely. According to the myth, he returned, after he taught the ceremonial to earth-surface apprentices, to his eight Coyote wives in the underworld.

From the foregoing explanation it would follow that the most important figures in the sandpaintings, in the healing and initiation effort, are the Coyote Girls. To begin with, the bodies of the two *yé'ii*-persons in any one direction are given the color which is appropriate for that direction. Eventually, however, the follower-*yé'ii* figures in the south, west, and north are given white body colorings on top of their original colors. So, for instance, the second *yé'ii* figure to the north, who can be seen in an earlier illustration as having a black dress, is now given a top coat of white. This extra labor is not a corrective for an earlier mistake—it is done so, consistently, in all four sandpaintings. And the singer sees to it that no step in the proper sequence was left out. What is the significance of this peculiar work sequence?

For quite some time, while I suspected pairs of a male and a female *yé'ii* for each direction, I labored under the impression that the additional white dresses signify femininity. Now that it is clear that all radial anthropomorphic sandpainting figures in this ceremonial represent Coyote Girls, an earlier statement of Luke Cook suddenly solves the problem much better. The follower-*yé'ii* figures who are given white dresses, together with the follower figure in the east which is white already, are daughters of the Talking-god. They must be dressed to match their father's appearance; he is the anthropomorphic white chief of the Navajo pantheon, in the east. Later we shall see that in live drama the female impersonator of one of these follower-*yé'ii* also wears a white dress. And so it seems, historically speaking, that the dresses of the follower-*yé'ii* figures from south, west, and north in the sandpainting were changed to white at the moment in history when the female impersonator was introduced, alongside the already white painted lead-*yé'ii*, to participate in the sacred mystery play.

Four horizontal red stripes on a blue ground color are standard neck markings on all anthropomorphic *yé'ii* figures. Two white strings and an eagle feather are always painted on their heads. Six eagle feathers are attached to the headgear and drape down the backs of all

...the second *yé'ii* figure to the north, who can be seen in an earlier illustration as having a black dress, is now given a top coat of white.

And the singer sees to it that no step in the proper sequence is left out.

the figures. Cords hanging from the elbows and hands of the *yé'ii*, traditional sleeve holders, are also standard features, together with the ears of corn in each of their hands. On the other hand, designs on their skirts are left entirely to the imagination of the individual sandpainter. Then finally, each directional region or home of the Coyote Girls is separated from the adjoining region by a maize plant. White maize grows in the southeast. Blue maize is represented in the southwest, yellow maize in the northwest, and black maize in the northeast— always in front of the lead-*yé'ii* of the same color.

corn colors

The sandpainting on the sixth morning differs from the previous one only in that no bowl is used at the center. A blue round patch of similar size is painted in its place. One man always starts to establish the center. For completing the remainder of the sandpainting team-work is the rule. The Rainbow-person is the last to be finished. He arches from his head in the northeast to his feet in the southeast. The opening to the entire microcosm is in the east—as is the entrance door to every Navajo hogan. The white Talking-god, chief of gods, rules from that direction.

On the seventh morning two features deviate from the sand-painting of the day before. The blue hole of emergence is given a

White maize grows in the southeast.

...on the sixth morning... no bowl is used at the center. A blue round
patch of similar size is painted in its place.

For completing the remainder of the sandpainting teamwork is the rule.

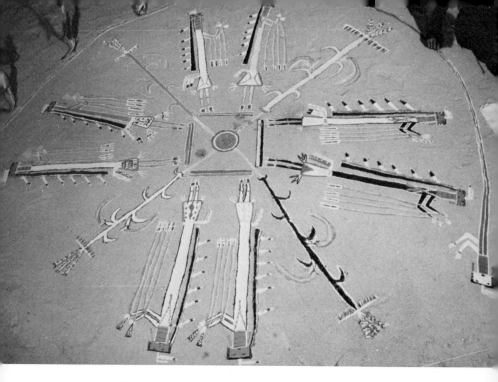

The Rainbow-person is the last to be finished.

rectangular shape—no particular reason could be given for this change. (Then, the northwest maize plant is replaced with a plant that has no maize ears. It represents all the plants on earth that provide prosperity for the animal peoples.)

No sandpainting is considered finished until at least thirteen Standing-up Prayersticks *(k'eet'áán ndii'á)* are stuck into the sand to surround the Rainbow-person who in turn encircles the miniature Coyote World. At the western end of the sandpainting the number includes two smaller Talking Prayersticks *(k'eet'áán yátti'ii)*. "All Standing-up Prayersticks do indeed talk," the singer explained, "it is only that additionally these two are named so." Below the two Talking Prayersticks a tool is deposited—a badger foot, bound together with other unnamed items from the Blessingway ceremonial. This tool is later used for erasing the sandpainting. Then, below the last Standing-up Prayerstick, nearest to the Rainbow-person's head, *kéttoh* bowl and *zaa'nit* shell are placed in readiness. A bundle of cedar twigs is added for use by the *yé'ii*-impersonator. When all these things are properly placed, and when the prayersticks can be seen in their standing-up prayer posture, the Sandpainting Ceremony has actually begun.

On the seventh morning… the blue hole of emergence is given a rectangular shape… the northwest maize plant is replaced with a plant that has no ears.

No sandpainting is considered finished until at least thirteen Standing-up Prayersticks are stuck in the sand….

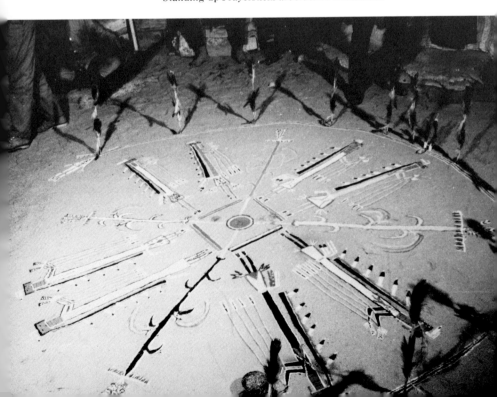

Below the two Talking Prayersticks a tool is deposited—a badger foot.

...*kétłoh* bowl and *zaa'nił* shell are placed in readiness.

THE CEREMONY

Compared with the length of time it takes to prepare the sand-painting, the duration of the *yé'ii* ceremony seems rather short. Everything is finished by the time the singer has chanted three songs. But, regardless of the brief time needed, this ceremony is pregnant with meaning. So, for instance, what the practitioner has given to the patient during the first four days, the *kétłoh* and *zaa'nił* medicines, are now administered by no lesser being than a Coyote Girl from the underworld—impersonated by a white-painted and blue-masked man. The ceremony is performed identically on the fifth, sixth, and seventh mornings of the ceremonial. Photographs in this report are from the first and second performances.

The ceremony begins when the practitioner places Standing-up Prayersticks in a circle. With these the microcosm of the sandpainting is sanctified and surrounded by a wall of prayer power. After *kétłoh* bowl, *zaa'nił* shell, and badger foot are in their proper places, the singer sprinkles pollen—first on the hole of emergence, then on the figures in the east, then on those in the west, next on those in the south, and finally on those in the north. Even the small rainbows around the central hole receive his attention. At last the all-surrounding rainbow is blessed from feet to head. Then, from a basket held by the patient, the singer sprinkles cornmeal—on all the sandpainting figures in the same sequence as with pollen. The patient, who is to be initiated, repeats the meal sprinkling after the example of his tutor.

These procedures endow the sandpainting with power of life. The sacred microcosm radiates its divine life essence and unites surface-world with underworld. Like attracts like, and before long a masked Coyote-person from the underworld appears.

The practitioner, however, rather than singing a song about a Coyote Girl's ascent to the surface-world—as would seem proper—sings about the original shaman's descent and arrival in the underworld of the Coyote People. This can only mean that presently this ceremony is being reenacted also in the underworld—or at least, that we relive here the original underworld ceremony. Whether we are ready for it or not, as participants in this ceremony we are all invited to "come down" with the original shaman, and with the patient, to the source of Coyote power:

86, 95, 101. Song, Fifth Through Eighth Mornings

From the Hogans I came down, from the Hogans I came down,
From the Hogans I came down, from the Hogans I came down.

...the singer sprinkles pollen—first the hole of emergence,
then the figures in the east....

Even the small rainbows around the central hole receive his attention.

Then, from a
basket held by the
patient, the singer
sprinkles cornmeal.

Like attracts like, and before long a masked Coyote-person
from the underworld appears.

From beneath the Two Rising I came down,
through the bushes I came down.
In the Hogan of White Coyote I came down,
through the bushes I came down.
On the White Medicine I came down,
through the bushes I came down.
On the Path of Cornpollen I came down,
through the bushes I came down.
On the Path of Rainbow I came down,
through the bushes I came down.
On the Path of Tobacco I came down,
through the bushes I came down.
On the Path of Corn-ripener Boy I came down,
through the bushes I came down.
From the Hogans I came down, from the Hogans I came down,
From the Hogans I came down, from the Hogans I came down.
From beneath the Two Setting I came down,
through the bushes I came down.
In the Hogan of Yellow Coyote I came down,
through the bushes I came down.
On the Yellow Medicine I came down,
through the bushes I came down.
On the Path of Cornpollen I came down,
through the bushes I came down.
On the Path of Sunshine I came down,
through the bushes I came down.
On the Path of Corn I came down,
through the bushes I came down.
On the Path of Yellow Tobacco I came down,
through the bushes I came down.
From the Hogans I came down, from the Hogans I came down,
From the Hogans I came down, from the Hogans I came down.
From beneath the Two I came down,
through the bushes I came down.
In the Hogan of Blue Coyote I came down,
through the bushes I came down.
On the Blue Medicine I came down,
through the bushes I came down.
On the Path of Pollen I came down,
through the bushes I came down.
On the Path of Sunshine I came down,
through the bushes I came down.
On the Path of Tobacco I came down,
through the bushes I came down.

On the Path of Rain I came down,
through the bushes I came down.
From the Hogans I came down, from the Hogans I came down,
From the Hogans I came down, from the Hogans I came down.
From beneath Where the Stars Turn I came down,
through the bushes I came down.
In the Hogan of Black Coyote I came down,
through the bushes I came down.
On the Black Medicine I came down,
through the bushes I came down.
On the Path of Pollen I came down,
through the bushes I came down.
On the Roots of Rain I came down,
through the bushes I came down.
On the Path of Corn I came down,
through the bushes I came down.
On the Path of Corn-ripener Girl I came down,
through the bushes I came down.
From the Hogans I came down, from the Hogans I came down,
From the Hogans I came down, from the Hogans I came down.

In the course of this song the masked Coyote impersonator appears. Straightway he goes to the *kétłoh* bowl and the *zaa'nił* shell. He takes the cedar twigs, dips them into both containers and sprinkles these medicines on the figures in the sandpainting. Sprinkling in the same east, west, south, north sequence, he endorses what the practitioner and his apprentice have done earlier. Each *yé'ii* figure in the sandpainting receives special attention—first the lead-*yé'ii*, then the follower-*yé'ii*, and then the maize plant of like color. After sprinkling he walks away with a howl:

Wu   wu   wu   wu   whoooo!

Now the patient enters the sacred microcosm. He sits on the western half of the sandpainting, facing the hole of emergence. Through this opening, everyone knows, the first human inhabitants have come into the surface-world. Through this same hole the first shamanic hero has gone down into the underworld to visit the holy Coyote People. Coyote power is communicated to men through the

He takes the cedar twigs, dips them into both containers
and sprinkles these medicines on the figures in the sandpainting.

Each *yé'ii* figure in the sandpainting receives special attention....

After sprinkling he walks away with a howl.

The Coyote-person reappears and presents the patient
with *kétłoh*… first to drink…

same orifice through which—to say it in the most personal manner—
Mother Earth has given birth to them. Healing and initiation in
Coyoteway implies a new birth.

The Coyote-person reappears and presents the patient with *kétłoh*,
rub-on medicine—first to drink and then to annoint the body. The
patient finishes rubbing on the medicine by himself. After this, the god
gives *zaa'nił*, the regular drinking medicine—first to drink and then to
rub on the body. In a somewhat possessive gesture the Coyote deity
applies this medicine to the head of the patient. Meanwhile, to docu-
ment the efficacy of the Coyote medicines, the singer is chanting the
story of the herbs from which these medicines are made:

87, 96, 102. Song, Fifth through Eighth Mornings

From the hidden Hogan I came with herbs,
From the hidden Hogan I came with herbs,
From the hidden Hogan I came with herbs,
From the hidden Hogan I came with herbs.
Beneath the Two Rising I came with herbs.
In the Hogan of White Coyote I came with herbs.
On the White Medicine I came with herbs....
(continued after the pattern of Song 86)

While this song is still in progress, the god returns with his cedar
twigs. He dips into the feet of the *yé'ii* figures in the eastern portion of
the sandpainting, also into the roots of the maize plants. With the
rough twigs he rubs the essences from the divine sandy feet onto the
feet of the patient. The god subsequently repeats this action with *yé'ii*
feet essences from the west, south, and north of the sandpainting. The
same harsh cedar twig treatment is repeated in three more rounds—for
body, breast, and head. After each such application the god moves
away from the patient in a sweeping motion; he exchanges the illness
for divine essences and throws it far away. With each such throwaway
motion the Coyote-god howls a "wu wu wu wu whoooo!" In conclusion of this procedure, and as a final act of taking possession, the
deity howls at close range into each of the patient's ears. For some
hours after this ceremony the patient remains silent. He seems visibly
shaken.

Before the divine Coyote leaves, he administers the Feather-
burning Rite. He brings the hot coal, sprinkles the feather mixture, and
rubs the strong-smelling smoke on the patient. Once more he impresses
his divine seal on the soul of the patient, by shouting into both of
his ears: "Wu wu wu wu whoooo! Wu wu wu wu whoooo!" Then he
goes outside.

The patient finishes rubbing on the *kétłoh* medicine by himself.

After this, the god gives *zaa'nił*, the regular drinking medicine.

In a somewhat possessive gesture the Coyote deity applies
this medicine to the head of the patient.

He dips into the feet of the *yé'ii* figures in the eastern
portion of the sandpainting....

...he exchanges the illness for divine essences and throws it far away.

...as a final act of taking possession, the deity howls at close
range into each of the patient's ears.

He brings the hot coal, sprinkles the feather mixture, and rubs
the strong-smelling smoke on the patient.

Shortly thereafter the *yé'ii*-impersonator reenters the hogan without wearing his mask. He quietly sits down in a corner as an ordinary
spectator. It is obvious that the real god has left and is now speeding
away outside. And with this god all the Holy People represented in the
sandpainting are beginning their departure. After a brief break the
patient leaves the sandpainting and goes outside.

[153]

With the god being gone, the singer assumes active leadership in the ritual. Sending home the Holy People from the east, he stoops down to wipe out with his badger foot the white lead-*yé'ii* figure, the follower-*yé'ii* figure, and then the figure of white maize. All the while he besings their departure:

88, 97, 103. Song, Fifth Through Eighth Mornings

Beneath the Two Rising, he ran.
With Early Morning Boy, he ran.
With Cornpollen for feet, he ran.
With the White Prayerstick for his hand, he ran.
With Early Morning for his feather, he ran.
With the Medicine in his hand, he ran.
With Happiness before him, he ran.
With Happiness behind him, he ran.
With Morning Dawn, he ran.

Sending home the Holy People from the east, he stoops down....

Then the singer moves on to send home the gods of the west.

Then the singer moves on to send home the gods of the west. He wipes out their figures and sings the second stanza:

Beneath the Two Setting, he ran.
With Yellow Twilight Girl, he ran.
With Cornpollen for feet, he ran.
With the Yellow Prayerstick for his hand, he ran.
With Evening Twilight for his feather, he ran.
With Yellow Air breathing from his mouth, he ran.
With Happiness behind him, he ran.
With Happiness before him, he ran.
With Evening Twilight, he ran.

Next he removes the pictorial presences of the gods of the south.

Next he removes the pictorial presences of the gods of the south. He sings the third stanza:

Beneath the Two Above, he ran.
With the Sunlight Boy, he ran.
With Cornpollen for his feet, he ran.
With the Blue Prayerstick for his hand, he ran.
With Midday Sunlight for his feather, he ran.
With the Medicine in his hand, he ran.
With Happiness before him, he ran.
With Happiness behind him, he ran.
With Midday Sunlight, he ran.

Finally he turns to the north and sends away the holy Coyote People of the underworld's north. As he wipes away their sandy representations he sings the fourth stanza:

Beneath Where the Stars Turn, he ran.
With the Darkness Girl, he ran.
With Cornpollen for his feet, he ran.
With the Black Prayerstick for his hand, he ran.
With Darkness for his feather, he ran.
With Night-air breathing from his mouth, he ran.
With Happiness behind him, he ran.
With Happiness before him, he ran.
With Darkness, he ran.

Finally he turns to the north and sends away the holy Coyote People
of the underworld's north.

Before the last stanza ends, the priest has taken out the emergence hole with its surrounding rainbows, he has also sent away the outer rainbow. Last of all, he gathers up the Standing-up Prayersticks—their prayers are spoken. This concludes the ceremony. While the patient still waits in the distance, two helpers enter and skim the colored sands from the top of the ruined sandpainting. All of it is scooped into a blanket and carried outside. The agents of illness which have been absorbed by these materials are so dumped in a remote place.

Last of all, he gathers up the Standing-up Prayersticks—
their prayers are spoken.

*The Three-*yé'ii *Ceremony*

THE SANDPAINTING

On the eighth morning the sandpainting differs from the preceding ones in a number of important features. It reintroduces the water bowl at the center. Then, two "rows" of maize plants are indicated between the four cardinal directions. Between these "rows" of maize are traced the trails which various Coyotes have taken to follow to the waterhole. According to *tséyi'nii* (see Chapter 10) the shamanic hero "came to a little pool of water with grass growing around it, and he saw that there were many tracks coming to the water, one from the south, one from the east, and one from the west. The track that he was following was from the north." The animal manifestations of the Coyote People who made the tracks can be seen in the sandpainting at the outer end of each trail. For assessing the Pueblo influence on Navajo cosmology it is interesting to note that the final portion of the road into the underworld is shown by the roots of maize plants.

Each lead-*yé'ii* in this sandpainting carries a stuffed animal-shaped Coyote-person. The six eagle feathers along the backs of the carried animals correspond to identical headgear arrangements on the anthropomorphic *yé'ii* figures. This establishes the identity of the animals with their carrier-*yé'ii* figures.

Behind the Coyote Carriers, in each of the four directions, the follower-*yé'ii* figures carry baskets. These baskets are spoked with eagle feathers and contain ears of maize.

A pair of these *yé'ii*-People, Coyote Girls, impersonated by a male who carries a stuffed gray fox and a female who carries a basket, will appear in person a few hours later. They will be attired to match their painted images. The art of sandpainting provides here the scenery for the performance of sacred drama. Both arts together serve to create the best situation in which the divine powers of the Coyote People can be mediated and where the initiatory healing event of mythical times is possible again.

THE CEREMONY

No new snow fell during the eighth night of the ceremonial, instead a hoarfrost decorates the landscape and low fog contours the rising sun. While the men, inside the hogan, have been occupied since 3 A.M. working on the last sandpainting, relatives of the patient are busy outside clearing a path toward the east. With the *yé'iibicheii*

On the eighth morning the sandpainting differs from the preceding
ones in a number of important features.

among them as their leader, everybody knows that the expected gods
will come from the east, on the path which is prepared for them.

At about 9 A.M. on the eighth morning the sandpainting is
completed. However, the singer withholds the feathered prayersticks, pollen, and meal. This means that the necessary preparations
are not all made for the ceremony to begin. As it turns out, many more
preparations are necessary on this special day.

The *yé'ii*-impersonators and their tutor go to the eastern end of the
path and erect there a wind shelter. To keep warm they build a fire.
At the very outset the practitioner puts moist sand into a gray fox skin
to soften it. Then all become occupied with rigging up their masks and
headdresses. Willow switches are cleaned of their bark and tied
together into frames for headdresses. Six eagle feathers are attached to
the draping portion of each Coyote Girl's headgear—in accordance
with the corresponding sandpainting figures. The mask of the Talking-
god is finished first. Then the Blue Coyote, the gray fox skin, is stuffed
with spruce twigs and with twigs from a chokecherry bush. Also, a
basket with radiating eagle feathers is made ready; white and yellow
ears of maize are bundled together with a spruce twig and laid into the
basket.

No new snow fell during the eighth night of the ceremonial, instead
a hoarfrost decorates the landscape and low fog contours the rising sun.

...relatives of the patient have been busy clearing a path toward the east.

The *yé'ii*-impersonators and their tutor go to the eastern end
of the path and erect there a wind shelter.

At the very outset
the practitioner
puts moist sand into
a gray fox skin
to soften it.

Willow switches are cleaned of their bark
and tied together into frames for headdresses.

Six eagle feathers are attached to the draping portion of each
Coyote Girl's headgear.... The mask of Talking-god is finished first.

Then the Blue Coyote, the gray fox skin, is stuffed with spruce twigs
and with twigs from a chokecherry bush.

Meanwhile, the priest cuts three reed prayersticks; he stuffs them
with tobacco and pollen dough as he did the earlier ones. They are
intended for the three *yé'ii* who will come. The female impersonator,
at the time still unmasked, "lights" these smoke-prayersticks with a
quartz crystal. For the time being the practitioner takes them into his
possession. And he sings:

117. Song, Eighth Morning

> *Hwii eiya eiya, he calls me.*
> *Hwii eiya eiya, he calls me.*
> *The Son of White Bead Lady I am, he calls me.*
> *The Clear Crystal Boy I am, he calls me.*
> *To the top of Blackbelted Mountain, he calls me.*
> *To the place where Rainbow arches, he calls me.*
> *The Talking-god Boy, he calls me.*
> *The Bluebird Feather, he calls me.*
> *Over Corn-ripener Beetle swaying treasures and pollen, he calls me.*
> *So his voice is made beautiful, he calls me.*
> *The song of Bluebird before me, he calls me.*
> *The sound of Corn-ripener Beetle behind me, he calls me.*
> *With Cornpollen at my feet, he calls me.*
> *Happiness before me, he calls me.*

Happiness behind me, he calls me.
The Long-life Happiness One I am, he calls me.
    Hwii eiya eiya, he calls me.
    Hwii eiya eiya, he calls me.

When all the gear of the *yé'ii*-impersonators lies ready, the practitioner bows to sanctify it with pollen. Following the singer's example all three impersonators sprinkle pollen on their gear—the *yé'iibicheii*-impersonator does it first. And while this happens the singer, thinking about who it is that will soon be touching the patient, chants two songs:

118. Song, Eighth Morning

White Bead Son is touching him.
    His voice is made beautiful.
Tips of Black Belts are touching him.
    His voice is made beautiful.
Floating Rainbow is touching him.
    His voice is made beautiful.
Talking-god Boy is touching him.
    His voice is made beautiful.
Young Bluebird Feather is touching him.
    His voice is made beautiful.
Many White Beads are touching him.
    His voice is made beautiful.
With his voice, He is touching him.
    His voice is made beautiful.
Beautiful valuable Things are touching him.
    His voice is made beautiful.
Beautiful Offerings are touching him.
    His voice is made beautiful.
Young Blue One is touching him.
    His voice is made beautiful.
Beautiful valuable Things are touching him.
    His voice is made beautiful.
Beautiful Offerings are touching him.
    His voice is made beautiful.
Beautiful Corn-ripener Beetle is touching him.
    His voice is made beautiful.
Cornpollen Girl is touching him.
    His voice is made beautiful.
Long-life Happiness One is touching him.
    His voice is made beautiful.

When all the gear of the *yé'ii*-impersonators lies ready, the practitioner
bows to sanctify it with pollen.

...all the three
impersonators
sprinkle pollen
on their gear—
the *yé'iibicheii*-
impersonator does
it first.

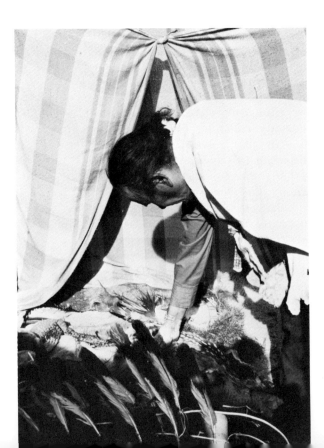

Happiness before, his voice is made beautiful.
Happiness behind, his voice is made beautiful.
The Long-life Happiness One I am.
The Beautiful Voice I am.

119. Song, Eighth Morning

The White Bead Son I am, it is given to me.
By the tips of Black Belts, it is given to me.
By the Floating Rainbow, it is given to me.
The Talking-god Boy I am, it is given to me.
By the Bluebird Feather, it is given to me.
By the Corn-ripener's pollen on my tongue, it is given to me.
With this, His voice, it is given to me.
With beautiful valuable Things, it is given to me.
With beautiful Offerings, it is given to me.
With the sound of Young Blue One before me, it is given to me.
With the sound of Corn-ripener behind me, it is given to me.
With Cornpollen for shoes before me, it is given to me.
  With Long-life Happiness One behind me, it is given to me.
  The Long-life Happiness One I am.
  With Happiness before me.
  With Happiness behind me.
  The Long-life Happiness One I am.

After these songs the practitioner bundles up the blankets on which the impersonators sat; they have in the process become his. Before he leaves he gives final instructions to the *yé'ii*-impersonators on how and where every action is to take place from here on out. Then he leaves the wind shelter and goes to the hogan where the patient awaits him. In the hogan he completes the sandpainting by adding standing-up prayersticks, badger foot, medicine bowl and shell at their usual places. Then he sits down at his regular place and faces the door.

Back east at the *yé'ii*-station the impersonators put on their costumes. Headdresses must be secured to the masks. Before long all stand ready to go.

The Talking-god, *yé'iibicheii* or Grandfather of the Gods, wears a buckskin over his shoulder and holds a fawnskin pouch with pollen in his hand. The bag-shaped white mask covers his entire head. A maize plant is painted on it in black along the line of his covered nose. Horsehair and eagle feathers crown the top of his head. A beard of spruce twigs surrounds his chin like a collar.

Blue Coyote Carrier wears the blue mask of Female God. This mask features a red-dyed and black horsehair top; a brown leather bib

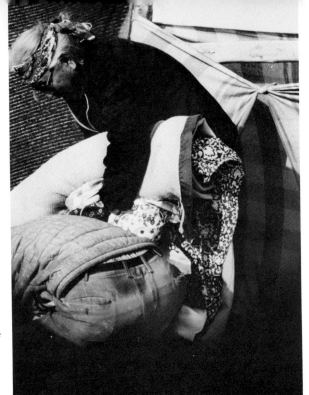

After these songs the practitioner bundles up the blankets on which the impersonators sat, they have in the process become his.

Before he leaves he gives final instructions to the *yé'ii*-impersonators.

Headdresses must
be secured to
the masks.

The Talking-god
wears a buckskin
over his shoulder
and holds a fawn-
skin pouch with
pollen in his hand.

Blue Coyote Carrier wears the blue mask of Female God.... Quite obviously, the Coyote Carrier and his Blue Coyote together constitute one being.

drapes around the chin. The facial features—triangular eyes, square mouth, and ladder-shaped nose—are outlined in black. Because of the cold weather the man is permitted to keep on his undershirt; his exposed body portions are, however, painted white. From his zigzag decorated kilt dangle eagle feathers. From his belt, behind, hangs a gray fox skin—the same kind as the stuffed animal which he carries under his arm. The Blue Coyote under the impersonator's arm wears along his back a headdress made of red-dyed horsehair; it contains the costumary six eagle feathers. Quite obviously, the Coyote Carrier and his Blue Coyote together constitute one being.

The third impersonator is a lady, wearing a festive white Navajo skirt and a dark velvet blouse. Her mask is identical to that of the Blue Coyote Carrier. She carries in her hands a traditional Navajo "wedding basket" with Pueblo Indian design. White and yellow ears of maize are in the basket, and eagle feathers are fastened to its sides.

The *yé'ii*-impersonators are lined up, ready to go. A few minutes pass. An awesome silence settles on the entire region. In everyone's breast excitement mounts as we are nearing the climax of the nine-day mystery play. The Talking-god impersonator lifts his mask to listen. When the singer's voice can be heard chanting from the hogan it is time for them to move on. Then, the gods can be seen moving toward the hogan, invited by the priest's song:

The third
impersonator is
a lady... her mask is
identical to that of
the Blue Coyote
Carrier.

The
yé'ii-impersonators
are lined up,
ready to go.

120. Song, Eighth Morning

Beneath the Two Rising he is moving, Coyote's corn is my corn.
In the White Corn he is moving, Coyote's corn is my corn.
Through the Snakeweed he is moving, Coyote's corn is my corn.

Beneath the Two Setting he is moving, Coyote's corn is my corn.
In the White Corn he is moving, Coyote's corn is my corn.
In the Yellow Corn he is moving, Coyote's corn is my corn.
Through the Snakeweed he is moving, Coyote's corn is my corn.

Beneath the Two Above he is moving, Coyote's corn is my corn.
In the White Corn he is moving, Coyote's corn is my corn.
In the Yellow Corn he is moving, Coyote's corn is my corn.
In the Blue Corn he is moving, Coyote's corn is my corn.
Through the Snakeweed he is moving, Coyote's corn is my corn.

Beneath Where the Stars Turn he is moving, Coyote's corn is my corn.
In the White Corn he is moving, Coyote's corn is my corn.
In the Yellow Corn he is moving, Coyote's corn is my corn.
In the Blue Corn he is moving, Coyote's corn is my corn.
In the Black Corn he is moving, Coyote's corn is my corn.
Through the Snakeweed he is moving, Coyote's corn is my corn.

Several times on their walk toward the ceremonial hogan, with the Wind People carrying the invitational song to the tips of their ears, the gods answer with their specific calls. Only the female impersonator remains silent. The Talking-god shouts:

Wu - u - whoooo!

The voice of the Coyote Carrier, a Coyote Girl, resounds with the already familiar:

Wu   wu   wu   wu   whoooo!

The Talking-god impersonator lifts his mask to listen.

Then, the gods can be seen moving toward the hogan,
invited by the priest's song.

As the three gods approach the hogan, the patient comes out to meet them. Standing on a buffalo skin he awaits their blessings.

Talking-god, with short dance steps, approaches the patient from the east; he gives his call and sprinkles pollen on him. Immediately after him, also from the east, approaches the Coyote Carrier; he raises his animal counterpart above the patient and gives his howl. Both *yé'ii*, the Talking-god and the Coyote Carrier, repeat their actions identically toward the Female God who at the time stands east of the patient. Why are Female God and patient treated alike? Is this rite reminiscent of the first shaman's marriage with his Coyote Girls in the underworld? Be that as it may. There is now no time to ponder. Events move fast when three gods reenact a divinely synchronized rite. After having blessed the patient from the east they move on to identically repeat their blessings from the south. A gap among the spectators opens up; it is possible now to capture on celluloid the last gesture of the Coyote Carrier in the south. The Talking-god is already moving on for his approach from the west.

This assembly of three gods has a human prompter. And prompters in all cultures are important people. Our good man has a remarkable talent for getting in front of my camera lens. He has clear ground to walk on, while I must jump about in two feet of snow if I wish to change my position. In spite of all this, he can not completely hide the Talking-god's blessings from above and from the west.

Only in their final round, when divine actions proceed from the north, do the gods answer the prayer of a photographer for a nice action sequence. From the north, again the Talking-god approaches the patient first and blesses him with pollen and a howl; after him Coyote Carrier comes and claims him by his call and by the blessings of his animal presence. A Female God at the periphery, again, shares in the patient's experience.

Inside the hogan, the singer has completed his song. The patient, the three gods, and their prompter enter the hogan for the final sand-painting ceremony.

At this point in the ceremony it is impossible for any spectator to enter the hogan. Earlier I had to make a choice to either be outside or be inside. After assuring myself that nothing new would happen inside I chose the outside. My choice proved to be the right one, especially in the light of what subsequently I could reconstruct through conversations. While the group is inside I will keep the tape recorder going by the door.

After the *yé'ii* enter the hogan, the animal Coyote is laid down on a blanket; his function has been fulfilled outside. The ritual inside is essentially the One-*yé'ii* Ceremony, a detailed description of which has

Talking-god, with short dance steps, approaches the patient from the east.

...he raises his animal counterpart above the patient and gives a howl.

After having blessed the patient from the east they move on
to identically repeat their blessings from the south.

A gap among the spectators opens up; it is possible now to capture
on celluloid the last gesture of the Coyote Carrier in the south.

...he can not completely hide the Talking-god's blessings
from above and from the west.

From the north, again the Talking-god approaches the patient
first and blesses him with pollen and a howl.

...after him Coyote Carrier comes and claims him by
his call and by the blessings of his animal presence.

The Female God, again, shares in the patient's experience.

The patient, the three gods, and their prompter, enter the hogan
for the final sandpainting ceremony.

already been given. It is not difficult to visualize the few minor
changes produced by the increased number of participating gods.

With the two Coyote Girls standing aside, the Talking-god
becomes active. He sprinkles pollen, cornmeal, and *kétłoh* medicine on
the figures in the sandpainting—on the lead-*yé'ii* in the east first, then
on the follower-*yé'ii*, and finally on the white maize plants. This
sequence is repeated—with pollen, cornmeal, and *kétłoh*—in the west,
the south, and the north of the sandpainting. All the while the priestly
singer chants a song in which he recognizes the presence of the Grandfather of the Gods. He also recognizes the happiness which the god is
bringing to all his divine and human grandchildren in the hogan:

121. Song, Eighth Morning

All is Happiness, all is well.
All is Happiness, all is well.
All is Happiness, all is well.
All is Happiness, all is well.
With the Talking-god's Children, all is Happiness, all is well.
With the White Beads, all is Happiness, all is well.
With the Black Prayerstick, all is Happiness, all is well.
With the Black Clouds, all is Happiness, all is well.

With the Lightning Flash, all is Happiness, all is well.
With White Bead Woman, all is Happiness, all is well.
With the Roots of Early Morning, all is Happiness, all is well.
With these He went. All is Happiness, all is well.
Over the Mountains. All is Happiness, all is well.
With Happiness He returned.
With Happiness He returned.
   All is Happiness, all is well—
   Now all is Happiness, all is well.
   Now all is Happiness, all is well.
With the Children of this Hogan, all is Happiness, all is well.
With the Children of Turquoise, all is Happiness, all is well.
With the Black Prayerstick, all is Happiness, all is well.
With the Black Clouds, all is Happiness, all is well.
With the Holy Medicine, all is Happiness, all is well.
With all Growing Plants, all is Happiness, all is well.
With Rain behind me, all is Happiness, all is well.
With many kinds of Turquoise, all is Happiness, all is well.
With Roots of Sunlight touching the mind, all is Happiness, all is well.
With Sunshine touching what lives, all is Happiness, all is well.
   All is Happiness, all is well—
   Now all is Happiness, all is well.
   Now all is Happiness, all is well.

After the Talking-god's blessings the patient sits down at his place on the sandpainting, west of the hole of emergence. Then the Coyote Carrier continues in the role of his counterpart from the One-*yé'ii* Ceremony. He puts *kétłoh* and *zaa'nił* medicines into the patient's mouth and rubs the remainders on his body—on feet, knees, breast, arms, back, and head.

While the female impersonator with her basket moves around the sandpainting to match the Coyote Carrier's directional activity, the latter takes sands from the feet of the *yé'ii* and the roots of the maize figures in the east of the sandpainting and applies them to the feet of the patient. This is repeated in an east, west, south, north sequence. The entire round is enacted for the patient's feet, knees, breast, arms, back, and head. Then four times the god touches with sand the tips of the patient's toes and four times his fingertips. In conclusion he puts pollen into the patient's mouth and howls into each of his ears. The songs chanted during these procedures are the same as in the One-*yé'ii* Ceremony:

122, 86, 95, 101. Song, Fifth Through Eighth Mornings

From the Hogans I came down, from the Hogans I came down,
From the Hogans I came down, from the Hogans I came down.
From beneath the Two Rising I came down, through the bushes....

123, 87, 96, 102. Song, Fifth Through Eighth Mornings

From the hidden Hogan I came with herbs,
From the hidden Hogan I came with herbs,
From the hidden Hogan I came with herbs,
From the hidden Hogan I came with herbs.
Beneath the Two Rising I came with herbs....

After these songs the Coyote Carrier administers the Feather-burning Rite. That being completed, the priest gives to each of the *yé'ii* the prayerstick which he prepared earlier. The impersonators are instructed to deposit them under a snakeweed plant.

When the *yé'ii*-impersonators leave the hogan, they take off their costumes and lay them, according to instructions, on a blanket "in the sun." There they dismantle their gear. With their intention to deposit

When the *yé'ii*-impersonators leave the hogan, they take off
their costumes and lay them... on a blanket "in the sun."

their prayersticks under a snakeweed plant, however, they face a problem. No such plants can be seen; with two feet of snow now on the ground only the tips of some tall weeds show. Eventually the resourceful practitioner advises them to keep the prayersticks until the snow melts; then the sticks should be placed in the appropriate manner, with a prayer.

While the *yé'ii* are leaving the hogan, the singer chants again the usual departure song. Coyote Carrier calls from all four directions of the sandpainting. Then, as in the preceding One-*yé'ii* Ceremonies, the singer wipes out the divine figures with his badger-foot tool and sends them home as they want to be sent home—with a song:

124, 88, 97, 103. Song, Fifth Through Eighth Mornings

Beneath the Two Rising, he ran.
With Early Morning Boy, he ran....

After the feathered prayersticks are taken off the floor, all the sand is carefully swept into a blanket and carried outside. Several loads of this are deposited at a distance from the hogan while the impersonators are still busy dismantling their gear. The Three-*yé'ii* Ceremony is now over. Before long everybody goes into the hogan for a festive meal. Only the summarizing of the basket-drum songs remains to be done during the next night; the climax of the nine-night ceremonial has just been passed.

Several loads of sand are deposited at a distance from the hogan
while the impersonators are still busy dismantling their gear.

Before long everybody goes into the hogan for a festive meal.

The Ninth-Night Summary

Beginning soon after midnight during the ninth night, the group of men rises and prepares for the final Basket-drum Ceremony. The Sandpainting Ceremonies have all been performed and the Holy *yé'ii*-People have come to bless and have gone again their ways. Now the task remains to sum up all the available blessings of the preceding nights. The patient returns to his regular place in the hogan; evidently it is no longer infectious. For a final medicinal measure in the ceremonial, yucca leaves are burned and given to the patient to drink, suspended in water. The cleansing power of yucca (soapweed) is so combined and put to work with the cleansing power of fire. All the basket-drum songs are repeated, full-length, on this last night. By the time all the songs are chanted a new day will be dawning in the east.

During the last of all the songs the patient again leaves the hogan. Then, while the singing continues, accompanied only by the rattle, the drumstick is taken apart. The now power-embued maize kernels are taken out and distributed among the participants. The place is swept and what little of the illness that might still have remained by this time is carried outside.

Eventually the patient returns. Everybody relaxes and is content. There is Happiness before us. There is Happiness behind us. The blessings of Talking-god and the holy Coyote People are floating all about us. "I feel real good, real good," says Luke Cook.

After our last breakfast together we all depart. The practitioner, who until now has maintained toward me the dignified distance required by his professional role, now clasps my hands and pats my shoulders for about a minute—perhaps the closest intimacy possible by Navajo custom among friends: *"Ya'at'eeh, Ya'at'eeh!"*—It is good, it is good! The Coyoteway is now recorded. It will not be forgotten.

Following a ceremonial of this magnitude, nothing is quite the same anymore for anyone among the participants—not to speak of the severe cold with which this ten-day camping trip has burdened me. The greatest transformation, however, is traditionally experienced by the patient. Initiated into the mysteries of the Coyote People, he has become a new person. His relationship to the Coyote-gods is evident by his new life-style. He must from here on out never harm a coyote, dog, fox, bobcat, badger, porcupine, or skunk. In his new relationship of close union with the holy Coyote People, these animals must now be considered his relatives. Moreover, he may no longer eat chokecherries because the branches and leaves of this bush have been used to stuff the fox skin for the final *yé'ii* ceremony. Eating these berries could be taken as eating his tutelary animal. Nevertheless, this same man is at the same time leaning toward acceptance of Christianity. It seems

All the basket-drum songs are repeated, full-length, on this last night.

appropriate therefore to provide the reader with a few glimpses of the greater ontological landscape in which his religious thinking presently may roam:

Mysticism, the ultimate religious posture which implies that man surrender his ego to be absorbed into a greater-than-human reality, is universally understood by religious people. Christian mystics become one with the universal Christ; Navajo Coyoteway singers and patients become one with the universal Coyote. The external differences among these two kinds of mysticism are related directly to the differences which exist among the concerns and fascinations in the traditions of monarchial herdsmen and primal hunters.

Coyote and his carnivorous relatives are predators—in relation to man they are fellow hunters and not sacrificial victims of the hunt. By contrast, the Christian savior is generally encountered within the thought structure of a sheepherder's world; he is the atoning and sacrificial Lamb of God. Coyotes eat lambs; and it is for this and other reasons that some Navajo Christians, shepherds, have concluded that Coyote is the Navajo devil. The counterpart to the Lamb of God in the traditional Navajo hunter religion is Deer (see Luckert 1975). The holy Deer People gave their flesh and blood sacrificially to the hunter ancestors of the Navajos.

Whether the Christian storyteller likes it or not, deity, in Navajo tradition, is revealed, among others, also in Coyote. God "appeared in flesh"—if you like—as a fellow hunter person. He stood his ground aggressively, after the manner in which Christ "barked at"—again if you like—the anti-human forces of his time. Christ stood his ground until he lost and was killed. In the eyes of some he was executed as an agent of the Devil; to the eyes of those who know better he has revealed himself as the heavenly Shepherd's sacrificial Lamb, sent for the salvation of humankind. Coyote, while insisting on his incarnate dignity as a fellow hunter person, was in the end himself hunted and killed. Coyotes, in predator-animal form, are killed because to some they appear to be agents of evil; from the perspective of those who know better, Coyotes must die in accordance with a procedure prescribed by Coyote gods, to furnish the paraphernalia and means for saving human patients.

In our post-hunting era many Navajo hunter gods have lost their influence over the people. Roaming now mainly among shepherds and planters, many have also lost their reputation with regard to being dependable savior gods. And so it seems the more remarkable that a rather pure hunter mysticism has survived to this day, intact, in the nearly extinct Coyoteway healing ceremonial. This book may, therefore, be compared to the efforts of a landscape painter who, enraptured by transhuman dimensions of beauty, is trying to sketch the

radiant play of colors in a cloudy sunset—before it all disappears. Coyoteway is the afterglow of a type of human fascination which long ago has been the property of all humankind. It is the shimmering light of an era along the human trail which is now fading into the dark recesses of forgotten aeons, carried along swiftly by the small currents of eternity.

For every sunset there is a sunrise. In the history of Coyoteway, as in the histories of many other Navajo ceremonials, this rising sun is the Talking-god, grandfather and chief of the pantheon. His leadership and supervision on the eighth morning puts authority behind the activities of the Coyote Girls. Then, at the moment when in the hogan the last song of Coyoteway ebbs away into silence, the Talking-god rises outside in his cosmic dimension as the White of Early Morning Dawn. Talking-god is an ancient anthropomorphic hunter tutelary who never appeared in animal clothes. The same divine-human process, which gives birth to Christ in a candlelit Christmas vesper, which lifts him from his tomb at an Easter morning sunrise, is what helps the solarized anthropomorphic Talking-god prevail against the wear and tear of time. He will outlive the animal revelations of the hunter era, of Coyote, and of his brothers and sisters.

PART THREE:

EARLY RECORDS
OF COYOTEWAY

Coyoteway Myth of
Yoo' Hataałii

"This myth was collected by Mary C. Wheelwright in 1931. It was given by *yoo' hataałii*, who lived near Ganado at that time. He learned the myth from *hastiin neez*, who lived, until his death in 1919, near Rainbow Bridge. *Yoo' hataałii* learned the Coyote Chant from *hashkéé náane* of Keams Canyon, Arizona." This information, and the myth, has been printed in Mary C. Wheelwright's *The Myth and Prayers of the Great Star Chant and the Myth of the Coyote Chant*, Santa Fe: Museum of Navaho Ceremonial Art, 1956. It is included here with the permission of the Museum of Navaho Ceremonial Art.

Paragraphs (1) through (8) contain materials that amount to an origin-myth for the Coyote Clan. The familiarity with the geography of the western portion of the Navajo Reservation suggests perhaps a late date.

Paragraphs (9) through (15) provide a realistic glimpse of shamanic possession. The Coyote Chant, the origin of which is described in this portion, appears to have been an Apachean prototype of the present Coyoteway ceremonial. The shamanic leader "walked into a rock," that is, he left the Earth-surface People. He appears later (in paragraph 23) as Messenger Wind to instigate the transfer of Coyoteway from the underworld. Thus, in this latter context, an old famous hunter shaman, already dead, lends authority to the by now Pueblo-influenced shamanic adventures of his grandnephew. This claim of a

[191]

younger shaman in transition is valid because in orthodox fashion he still "grew up and liked nothing but hunting." Paragraphs (16) and (17) set the stage for obtaining a Pueblo-influenced version of Coyoteway back in Old Navajoland.

Paragraphs (18) through (24) describe the younger shaman's journey into the underworld. "A ladder sticking out of the water" (22) is obviously related to Pueblo *kiva* architecture and to the mythic flood caused by the Water Serpent. This myth can be traced all the way to the Olmec strata of Middle American civilization.

Paragraphs (25) through (35) narrate the acquisition of Coyote-power by the shamanic hero. He learns about his relationship with the Coyote People of the underworld. He eats Coyote food—and in the process traces the origin of corn to the Coyote People. Credit for corn is so given to Apachean tutelary deities instead of to mortal Pueblo Indians. Finally the shaman marries eight Coyote Girls. Having thus become a full Coyote-person himself, the shaman is entrusted with the Coyoteway ceremonial.

Paragraph (36) tells about the shaman's return to the surface-world after four years. He taught Coyoteway to his younger brother who in turn taught it to others. Learned priests, professionals, performed the Coyoteway ceremonial from that time on. The first Coyoteway singer, however, still a genuine shaman, has himself crossed the threshold of ordinary human existence. He is now a Coyote-person and therefore obligated to live with the Coyote People in the underworld.

(1) The story begins on an island in the western ocean when Changing Woman decided to make more people.[1] This was after her sons, Monster Slayer and Born-for-Water, had killed the monsters who were destroying mankind. She bathed herself in a white shell and dried herself with white corn and yellow corn. Then she took the water in which she had washed and emptied it into the sea. A fog arose, and the white shell and white corn drifted together and made people. They came into existence and their name was the *yoo'i dine'é* or Bead People, named after the white shell out of which they were made. The first two men were made of white corn, and the first two women of white corn; then were made two men of yellow corn and two women of yellow corn; after this were made two white corn boys and girls, and two yellow corn boys and girls.

(2) Changing Woman told these people that they must go east-

---

[1]Wherever possible, the Navajo transcriptions of the original author have been brought into conformity with current practice. Unchanged transcriptions are given with quotation marks. The names of some well-known personages are given in English rather than in Navajo.

ward. The Yellow Corn People traveled on the black cloud and the White Corn People on the gentle rain. The black cloud and the gentle rain guided them across the sea until they got to *naadą́ą́' dził* or Corn Mountain, where they spent the night. Then they went on to *dził tł'ah deel'áii* and spent a second night there. Afterwards they traveled to the second mountain, *dził n'deel'áii*, then to the third mountain, *dził tah deel'áii*, and to the fourth mountain, *dził dinilt'é*, and spent a night at each mountain. On the fourth mountain the white-corn First Man woke at dawn and said that he had had a dream. He told his people that it was a holy dream and that it was the beginning of his ceremony. On this same night the yellow-corn First Man had a dream and told his people about it and said that he knew something was going to happen. The dream of the White Corn man was that he was flying with wings, and he was the originator of the *yoo'*, or Bead, Chant. The Yellow Corn man dreamed that he turned into a white coyote, and that his power came from *nááts'íílid*, the Rainbow. After they had told their dreams the people went on to *niłtsá dził*, Rain Mountain, and slept there, and then to another Corn Mountain, and then to *nanise' dził* which means Vegetation Mountain. Then they traveled on to *tádídíín dził*, Pollen Mountain. There the White Corn man dreamed again, and at dawn told his people that he had dreamed of being very high up near a sky world. Yellow Corn man dreamed that he was walking toward the east with four rainbows around him, and he said he thought everything would be all right on the journey.

(3) They traveled on and came to *yódí dził*, Soft Goods Mountain, and slept there. Then to *ntł'iz dził*, Jewel Mountain, and then to *tsin beel'á*, Trees-growing-on-the-side-of-mountain, and there they talked about their dreams and wondered why the dreams had come to them. "Does it mean that we must go back, or that we should make offerings to the gods?" And they decided to have the ceremony of *hóshǫ́ǫ́jí*, or Blessingway, over some offerings of turquoise, jet, abalone, and white shell. They all made these offerings to Changing Woman and had the Blessing Ceremony over them. They also gave the Blessing Ceremony over the two head men, the White Corn man and the Yellow Corn man. This was the beginning of this ceremony, and after they had finished it they were not worried any more about their dreams and felt that all would be well on their journey. All the songs used at that ceremony belonged to *nihosdzáán* or Mother Earth.

(4) Then they went on and came to *dook'o'osłiid*, San Francisco Peaks, and went up to the top whence they could see in every direction. At the north they saw rain far off and at the east a rainbow. The White Corn man wanted to go towards the rain at the north and Yellow Corn man towards the rainbow. At this place they began to differ in their plans and Yellow Corn man gave White Corn man his

ceremonial name and White Corn man did the same for Yellow Corn man. Yellow Corn man spoke to the White Corn man, calling him "Tsah Oshkinzh" and said, "I think we should go towards the rainbow at the east, for if we take this road we would have abundance." White Corn man then spoke to Yellow Corn man and said, "I never thought that you would disagree with me, 'Tsinh Hodekloch'."

(5) After this the people went towards the rain at the north and came to *dził łibái*, Gray Mountain, and found there many kinds of bushes with berries: "hashjeh-tanh (coyote bush)," also *tł'oh ts'ósí* and *tł'oh tsoh* and "degliddi" which has seeds good to eat. White Corn man told his brother, "We were right in taking this path to the north, if we had taken your path we would have had nothing to eat." Then they decided to get on to *dził diłhił*, Darkness Mountain. When they came there, there were many animal people: all members of the lion and cat families, *náshdóítsoh*, the Mountain Lion and his people. White Corn man dreamed in this place that he was to be one of these lion people and Yellow Corn man dreamed that he was to be of the *mạ'íi* or Coyote family. Then they went on to *tó naneesdizí*, Tangled or Intertwining Water (Leupp), where there is a peak, and there they found more animal people of the lion and coyote families, and went on to "Nastin-tsonh," a peak near Black Mountain, where they met more animal people. The people lived on the seeds of plants on their journey.

(6) Then they went to *naatsis'áán*, Navajo Mountain, and they stayed four years on the top of the mountain. There were all kinds of food there to eat: *didzé dit'ódí, chiiłchin, łichí'í*, "nahtezh," *tł'oh tsoh, tł'oh ts'ósí*, "degliddi," and *tł'oh chí'í*. Some of the people went hunting to the north for deer, mountain sheep, and other animals. They found they had to go a long way to get the meat, and finally decided to move on further and went along a ridge to a place later called *aghaa' łáni*. They stayed in this place four years and hunted, and towards *déni-hootso* they found antelope and drove them into traps in the canyons. They named this place *aghaa' łáni*, Much Wool, because after cleaning the skins there was much hair and wool accumulated in that place. They made clothes for themselves there.

(7) Finally the game began to grow scarce and they decided to move on again. So they went towards Black Mountain to *to díneesh-zhee'* and from there to *baa' lók'a'í* north of White Cone, Arizona. There they looked about, and they could see at the northeast the Luka-chukai Mountains, and the White Corn man said he was going in that direction to follow the rain in valleys. Then they looked towards the east and saw a rainbow towards *tséyi'*, Canyon De Chelly, and Yellow Corn man said he would go that way. So at this place the brothers separated. Yellow Corn man, the younger brother, spoke to his older brother and said, "You go your way to 'Tsah-ash-ezh' and take your

family with you," and the older brother told his younger brother that he should follow his own way with his family towards *tséyi'* Canyon.

(8) The White Corn man and his family came to a place called *taah eelk'id*, Ridge-which-goes-into-the-water (ten miles north of Chinle), and these people were the originators of the Bead Chant. The people of the Yellow Corn went to a place called *tsé binááz'éli* at the mouth of *tséyi'* Canyon, and found there many bushes full of berries growing up the canyon, and also there were many bears among the bushes. The White Corn People who went to the north found a lot of seed plants also, and at about sundown they came to *taah eelk'id*. There they ground up the seeds and made bread and balls of ground seeds. They ate these before dark and set some before the leader. Also just before dark the Yellow Corn People in the canyon gathered seeds particularly from *ma'iidą́ą́'*, or coyote bush, and ground this to meal and set the food before their leader. The White Corn man said as his food was set before him, "I wonder what my brother is doing tonight. If he were with us he would have plenty to eat, but I am afraid by this time his stomach is trembling with hunger." At the same time his younger brother was making the same remark about him. So the White Corn and the Yellow Corn People separated. Each went their own way and they did not meet again.

(9) The leader of the Yellow Corn or Coyote People and his wife made their fire at a distance from the camp of their family. That evening the Coyote People began to wonder why their leader had not told them where to go the next day, and they said, "He does not seem to care for us." They supposed their leader was asleep, though his fire was still burning. Just as they were dropping asleep they heard their leader singing, the first Coyote song. The family talked about this song, as they did not know it, and said, "All through our journey we have never heard him sing before, and he would always build his fire apart with his wife and never told us that he could sing." No one dared go to the leader, and they finally went to sleep. Early in the dawn the people woke and looking towards *tsé binááz'éli* they saw a *yé'ii* (god) standing facing east. Then they realized that it was their leader and they said, "What is he doing there so early in the morning? Why is he acting like a child?"

(10) Just then he jumped off the rock and came back to his fire from another direction. No one had spoken a word to the leader but now they went to him and asked him why he had sung and why he had been up on the rock. They said, "Are you a child to behave so? You might fall off, you must not do this, but take care of us and be our leader." He said, "My children, I am not behaving like a child. The place where I was at dawn was a holy place. I left my footprints on top of the rock and in times to come our people will pray there and make

offerings when they are in distress or need. Help will be given them, and will never fail. I did this for you and for our people to come."

(11) The people talked this over and said they wanted to go on, for they were afraid that their leader might do something strange again. He had brought with him something given by Changing Woman called *tł'iish k'aa'*, Arrow Snake, and he carried this as they went up the canyon to a place called *tsé ninootł'izh* where there are now zigzag white marks on the rocks. They made camp opposite this place. They built two fires, one for the leader separate from the rest. He came to their fire that night and they talked about where to go and where to get food. They asked his advice. He said, "My children, I am leaving it to you. Up to this time I have been leading you but I have something else now that I must do." Then he went back to his own fire and the people talked together. When they were ready to go to sleep they heard the leader singing again.

(12) When they woke at dawn they saw him climbing on the cliff opposite. He made the zigzag marks there and sang a song of the *yé'iibicheii*, and then came back to his own fire as before. The people went to him and asked him why he behaved in this way, and he said, "My children, the place is holy and I left my marks on it, and I left also all that Changing Woman gave me. In time to come when people are in trouble and need rain they should make offerings at this place and they will get what they need. This is why I have done it." But the people did not seem to understand and were suspicious, and talked about where they wanted to go, and said, "If he keeps on doing these things we might lose him."

(13) Then they went along up the canyon and came to a place now called *ch'ó haazt'i'*, Fir-trees-growing-in-row-at-mouth-of-canyon. They camped opposite this place, and made two fires as before. The people went to the leader's fire and asked him what he was going to do now, and he said, "My children, I am not doing these things of my own accord. Since we left Changing Woman to go on our own journey I have been given these things to do and my actions come to me from a holy place." In the night the people talked it all over and said, "During our journey from the island we never heard him sing, but at various times he had dreams. For these dreams we have already had a Blessing ceremony and have given offerings, but it did not seem to do us any good." They said to the leader again, "You must take care of us," and they asked him again what made him behave in this way. He said, "My children, I cannot behave differently because I have given myself up to the Holy Ones already."

(14) The people talked half the night and heard the leader singing as before, and at dawn they saw him standing on a cliff across the little

canyon. They heard him give a song of *haashch'ééłti'í*, the Talking-god, and then he jumped down into the canyon. Where he stepped, fir trees sprang up in his footprints, and this gave the name to this place. Then the leader came back to his fire and they questioned him again, and he said, "Don't you believe what I told you before? I have given myself to the Holy People and I won't be long with you. I am doing this for you and the people to come. In the future I will be with you always and will appear in different forms. You have been talking about me for three nights, but after this fourth night you will see me no more."

(15) He told them now for the first time that he was selected by the Holy Ones to give the Coyote Chant, and said, "In the future, when there are lots of people on earth, if they do not give the Coyote Chant they will not live happily. My dreams told me this. In the future when there is drought the White Coyote of the east will howl, for then all the coyotes over the earth will howl, calling the rain for the people." Then they went on their journey in the canyon and came to *tsé nteel* and camped nearby, and everything happened as before except that the leader did not sing that night. Early at dawn they saw him again on the top of the cliffs and this time he was dressed as Talking-god. He sang and then jumped off the cliff and came up to their fire and pulled off his mask so that they could see that it was their leader. He said, "This is the last time you are going to see me now. I am going to stay in this canyon forever. You, children, can go on your way and take care of yourselves and go where you like." After these words he turned around and walked toward *tsé nteel* and as he went he sang *yé'iibicheii* songs. Then he walked into the rock.

(16) The people took another leader, the nephew of the first leader, and went up Lukachukai Mountain and spent the night there. They talked about the first chief, saying that he had gone to a holy place. His wife was with them. Next day they picked seeds for food and crossed the mountain and went down to *tsé łichíí' dah azkání*, a tall rock now called *chí'ídi* in Red Rock Valley. They got there at sundown and spent the night. Then they went toward the San Juan River to *taah dootł'izhí*, Blue-land-goes-into-river, where the Animas and San Juan rivers meet in the direction of *dził ná'oodiłii*, Huerfano Peak. They came to that blue land and stopped to pick seeds and spend the night. From there they went on by a ridge leading to *dibéntsaa*, La Plata Mountains, and spent the night there, and passed by *tó ts'ósíkooh*, Narrow-water-canyon, where there were people living in the cliffs. If they had seen them the story would have been different.

(17) Then they went on top of *dibéntsaa* and spent the night there and at midnight a rainbow appeared over them which was a sign that they should follow it and in the morning it went towards the east.

When the first leader left he told them that he would always be with
them and when this rainbow appeared they knew that he was with
them. The leader had told them that this was the first sign that he
would show them. The rainbow went before them to *ch'olyáázh ashkii*
at the east of the La Plata Mountains. They stayed there four years,
and there the nephew of the present leader married the first leader's
wife and their children began another family. They had eight children, four boys and four girls, and they were all born two years apart.

(18) The oldest of these boys when he grew up liked nothing but
hunting. He learned the ways of hunting deer, rabbits, mountain
sheep, squirrels, and antelope, and he was so keen about hunting that
he hardly slept. His only weapons were bows and arrows and he spent
his nights making them and putting piñon gum on the bows and
polishing the arrows. He started at dawn on the mountains and at sundown would bring in the game, for his father was growing quite old
and depended on him more and more. For four years he hunted. (Up
to this point, the myth is similar to the version collected earlier from
"Tsegi-ruhe" by Mary C. Wheelwright.)

(19) One night in *niłch'itsoh*, the Great-Wind-Month—December,
about an inch of snow fell. The young man stayed up all night for he
wanted to start very early to go trapping, and he left for the hunt
before dawn. He went towards *dibéntsaa* but could not find game. He
got lost, and when night came he went into a little cave and took cedar
boughs to cover him. Very early in the morning he started again and
came to "Tsen-koh-oltsin" just before sun-up, and saw a coyote track
and followed it.

(20) Meanwhile his parents were very much worried because he
usually came home every night. They thought he must have frozen or
had been eaten by some beast and they did not sleep. His father started
in the early morning to try and track him down, but as the sun rose the
snow melted and there were no tracks. His father searched for him four
days and then gave it up as hopeless, but his son was alive.

(21) After the hunter found the coyote track he followed it because
he hoped that the coyote might have chased a rabbit into a hole and he
would be able to catch it. After a time he stopped and decided to back-
track the coyote and came to a canyon where he saw a coyote coming
down the other side of the canyon. He went down into the canyon at
about sunrise and at the bottom he found the coyote's sign or spoor.
Looking at it closely he saw that it was fresh and that there was a
kernel of hard white corn in it, and he wondered where this came from
in the middle of the winter. He went on backtracking the coyote until
he came to a flat place where there was a round pond, covered with
ice, with bulrushes growing round it, and he saw that the tracks of the
coyote came out of this pond on the east side. He tried to find where

the coyote had lain down or where he had come from so he went all around the pool of ice but only found tracks coming out of it. Then he circled the ice again in a bigger circle and on the west side he found another track leaving the ice, and following this track he found another piece of hard yellow corn, in the spoor. He went back to the ice again and found tracks coming out of it at the south, and following this track he found blue corn in the spoor. He went back to the ice again and took his bow and searched in the bulrushes. He found other tracks at the north with black corn kernels in the spoor.

(22) Then he stood at the east of the pool and took his bow and tried to lift up the ice, but it would not move. He tried it from the west, the south and the north, but he could not move it. So he tried again at the east side and the ice lifted. He saw a ladder sticking out of the water underneath.

(23) He wanted to go down the ladder but thought he would freeze, it seemed so cold. Then *niłch'i biyáázh* (who was the first leader in the form of Messenger Wind) spoke to him and said, "The water is just a covering to the hole. Blow with your breath on it and you can go down." So the hunter blew four times on it and the water went away to one side, and he looked and saw there were four ladders, one below the other, leading down. So he climbed down the four ladders and as soon as he arrived at the bottom the water closed up overhead.

(24) He turned to the east and saw fields of white hard corn, and turned to the west and there were fields of yellow corn. At the south there were blue cornfields and at the north, black. At the east there was a long white house, at the west a yellow one, at the south a blue one, and at the north a black one. And he saw smoke coming out of the houses and heard the sound of children's voices coming from all of them. He said to himself, "What is this world that I am in? I wonder if these people will be kind enough to feed me?" And he did not know which house to go to. He listened and at the east he heard what the people were saying. The children were roasting corn, and as it popped the children said, "Mah-ih desah," for they were Coyote People. And then he heard these same words coming from all directions.

(25) So he went to the white house at the east and on entering it he saw a man colored white who said, "Where did you come from, son-in-law, here is no place for Earth People." The hunter told him his story and that he came to find out where the corn had been found in the winter. The Coyote man said, "The tracks that you saw were those of my son going out hunting and it is nearly dark now and he will come back soon. We have heard about your people who came from the island of Changing Woman, and we also know about the first dream that your chief had, this dream was about our Coyote People. The White Coyote that your first chief dreamed about was my son."

(26) Then they made a place for the hunter at the west side of the house, and the Coyote man began to tell the hunter the story of the Coyote People, saying that they came from Changing Woman long ago. He also said, "Now I see that you come from her also and that you are *yoo' diné*, Bead People." Then the Coyote man told the hunter the story of the journey of his own people and about how the first chief was taken by the gods at *tséyi'*. He told him that the first chief had spoken to the hunter in the form of the Messenger Wind and had led him to the Coyote People. He said that when the first chief was going to leave his people he told them that he would be with them in different forms. The hunter did not know these things. The Coyote man told the hunter about his people and everything that had happened to him since his birth, and said when he finished, "Now I will make you holy."

(27) At midnight one of the Coyote's sons who had been out hunting toward the west came into the house. He had small game of different kinds with him and they placed it spread out on a sacred doe skin placed on the ground with the head to the east. He said to the hunter, "My son-in-law, you must watch closely what we are going to do now." The young Coyote man who had brought in the game took a small object from his belt and laid it on the skin and said to the hunter, "This is what we get when we go hunting on the earth, and the Earth People pursue us because of this." Then they spread a buckskin on the top of the game with the small object on it, and they all stood at the east of the skin and stepped over it to the west and back again, meanwhile making coyote sounds. The hunter watched carefully and saw that the buckskin began to move. Then the Coyote People stood at the west side and stepped over the skin towards the east and back again, and the buckskin rose higher. Then the Coyote People stood at the south and stepped to the north and back, and the skin rose higher still. Then they stood at the north and stepped toward the south and back, and by this time the hunter could see what was underneath the skin. It was a mass of fat. The Coyote man told the hunter that this had grown from the tiny piece of fat which was brought back by the Coyote hunter, and that this fat came from all the food animals belonging to the Earth People and made lean by the pursuit of coyotes. Then the Coyote People uncovered the fat which came from the deer and other game, and all the other Coyote People that lived in the blue, yellow, and black houses came and ate some of the fat and then went back to their own homes. The Coyote man told the hunter that this was the way in which they ate, and for this reason Earth People do not like coyotes.

(28) He said, "We will give you something to eat also." So he sent two of his beautiful daughters into the cornfield toward the east. They brought home four ears of corn and roasted three on the fire and set

them before the hunter. He ate the three ears of corn and kept one. The Coyote man said, "When you get back to the earth take that ear of corn with you and plant it and you will always be able to live on it and increase." After the hunter had eaten this corn they told him again the story of the journey of his own people, and the Coyote man said, "Now you have eaten and learned the history of your people. And now you can sleep, and I will give you both of my daughters." The hunter and the Coyote girls slept together.

(29) At dawn the next morning both the girls left the hunter and he could overhear their talk with their father in the next room. The father asked whether the hunter had been good to them and they said he was a good Earth Man. Later in the morning the Coyote man told the hunter not to go too far away to hunt and to take care of his two wives. He said to be careful, as there were lots of bad people about. And he said, "After you have been with us a while longer you can go your own way."

(30) The hunter disregarded the warning and went a long way off to the yellow house at the west, and there he found the Yellow Coyote People. They asked him to spend the night there. The chief said that one of his sons was out hunting and was about to come back, and that he wanted the hunter to see what his son would bring. Then Yellow Coyote man told the hunter about the history of his family. After dark the son came in, and they had the same feast of fat as in the east house and also the hunter was given four ears of yellow corn. He ate three ears and kept one to be planted in the earth. He married two Yellow Coyote girls there and in the morning they told their father that he was a fine man.

(31) The Yellow Coyote man warned him not to go further and to take care of his daughters, but again he wandered away and spent the next night at the Blue Coyote's house in the south, where they had the same ceremony of eating the fat. Then he was given four ears of blue corn and kept one to plant on the earth, and he also married two Blue Coyote girls.

(32) The next day he went to the black house at the north, where the same things happened: the eating of the fat, his eating of the corn and keeping one ear to plant on earth, and the marrying of two Black Coyote girls. He also learned how to make images of the coyote for offerings.

(33) Later he went to the yellow, blue, and black houses and learned their *k'eet'áán* offerings there. He also learned the *wooltááá* ceremony in each of the houses. After he had learned about the ceremonies the Coyote man said, "You have learned everything that we know and before you go we should like to give you the medicine and the pouch for it." So at the east house a five-night ceremony was given

for the hunter; this consisted of *k'eet'áán* offerings, but no sand-paintings were made. For five nights they painted the hunter red, spotted him with double white spots all over, and tied a feather to his hair. The Yellow Coyote man at the western house gave a nine-night ceremony for him which included the sweating ceremony inside the hogan every morning for four days and afterwards sandpaintings for four days. Nowadays on three nights in this ceremony the patient is treated in the *wooltáád* ceremony by someone wearing a *yé'iibicheii* mask (should perhaps read "*yé'ii* mask"). On the last night the patient stands on a buckskin holding ground meal in a basket and three gods, Talking-god, Coyote, and Female God come to the patient, and Female God holds a shell with cornpollen in it and four eagle tail feathers radiating from the center.

(34) After this ceremony the Blue Coyote man in the south house gave a five-night ceremony over the hunter like the one in the east house. Then the Black Coyote man of the north gave a nine-night ceremony over him, and after this they all gave him their masks and medicine, and gave him his ceremonial name, "Nakoholdehe," which is a holy name. (There never was a public dance at the end of the Coyote's ceremony.) After this he was ready to leave and they told him that when he got back to his people he must teach one of his brothers everything that he had seen and learned. They said "You must have a ceremony over your brothers, and from now on all Earth People should have these ceremonies."

(35) The four ears of corn that he had kept he took with him for the Earth People, and out of this corn they made the images of four coyotes and one dog that are used in the ceremony. There are eight white *k'eet'áán* for the east, eight blue for the south, eight yellow for the west, and eight black for the north, and one image of Coyote for each direction. At the north is a black image of a dog and a black *k'eet'áán*. The dog is called *łééchąą'í*, and at his left a pellet of *biyeel*, sacred offering, should be placed. There should be four yellow-headed black-bird feathers radiating in the four directions. All these offerings are to be made in the hogan and then taken out and placed outside of it, and they should be made before the first fire is made each day.

(36) After he had learned all this, the hunter went back to his people and gave the corn to his father and mother. He had thought that he had been away a very short time but found that he had been gone four years. Then the Earth People began these ceremonies, and the hunter gave all his knowledge to his younger brother. He gave a ceremony over him and told the people not to forget what they had learned and to always give the ceremonies. He said, "I am going to leave you, you are seeing me for the last time." Then he went back to his wives and the Coyote People.

Coyoteway Myth of
Tséyi'nii

The names of the recorder and/or editor of the manuscript of this myth are uncertain. Perhaps Laura Armer is alone responsible for its existence; perhaps Mary Wheelwright had something to do with it. Or, a remote possibility is that even Father Berard was involved in some capacity. Permission to print has been obtained from the Museum of Navaho Ceremonial Art, Santa Fe, as well as from the Franciscan Missionary Union, Cincinnati, Ohio. The manuscript was prefaced with the following note:

"Ma-ihji Hatral (Coyote Story), told at Mrs. Armer's House at Black Mountain, October, 1934, by Tsegi-ni, 75 years old, who comes from Canyon De Chelly, and who was born three years before the time when the Navahoes were taken to Bosque Redondo. Interpreted by Tse-na-jinnhe (Taylor)."

Paragraphs (1) through (3) describe the shamanic hero's descent into the underworld. Paragraph (4) briefly reports about his learning of Coyoteway. Paragraph (5) sketches the transition of the ceremonial's performance from the shaman to subsequent practitioners.

In paragraph (6) the narrator's thoughts wander to a pair of gods which exceed the Coyote People in authority and power: they are the Talking-god and the Calling-god. The point seems to be that both gods had coyotelike dog children.

Paragraph (7) reports a repeat journey into the underworld for the purpose of obtaining more ceremonial information.

Paragraphs (8) through (12) narrate the episode of Coyote's visit at the place of Horned Toad. See Luke Cook's version in Chapter 2.

Paragraphs (13) through (20) contain stories about the "trotting" and "adulterous" Coyote. The series begins with Coyote meeting the Sliding Lizards, an episode referred to in Song 74.

Paragraphs (21) through (28) tell the story of Coyote's marriage to the Changing Bear Woman—a theme from Evilway-type Upward-reaching mythology. Evilway mythology regards Coyote as the epitome of evil which must be killed or driven away. Luke Cook, in Chapter 2, transforms the story into a Holyway-type origin myth of Coyoteway: Coyote is not an evil being, rather, he is a patient in need of the first Coyoteway ceremonial. The present story, still an apologetic one, tries to save Coyote by portraying him as a foolish but harmless gambler—a weakness which no Navajo will count against him. Curiously, the Fire Ceremony or the Feather-burning Rite is here not administered to Coyote, as Luke Cook (Chapter 2) has it; rather, Changing Bear Woman is the patient, and the witchcraft arrows are removed from her body. Thus, in paragraphs (21) through (28), where attention is shifted to the Bear Woman, Coyote is in the process of becoming disassociated from Evilway mythology. If the final episode in *tséyi'nii*'s myth is evaluated in this manner, it seems as though his paragraphs (13) through (20) have already been part of his apologetics—Coyote is being pushed to the periphery of Evilway thinking as a harmless bungler. In paragraph (26) *tséyi'nii* tries to disassociate the "trotting" and "adulterous" Coyote from the origin of the Coyoteway ceremonial. This particular solution is, however, in direct contradiction with Luke Cook's story, also with references to the "adulterous" and the "staggering" Coyote in some songs of the now recorded Coyoteway ceremonial. But then, apologetics is never systematic theology.

(1) The story begins at *tséyi'ii* (Mesa Verde) near *dibéntsaa* where the son of *jóhonaa'éí* was living.[1] His name was "Nalth-keh-olth-eh." It was early in the morning and snow was falling, and when he walked out on the snow he saw a Coyote track and followed it, knowing that the Coyote was probably following rabbits which he wanted to get. He did not know which way it would be best to follow the track, but

---

[1]Wherever possible, the Navajo transcriptions of the original author have been brought into conformity with current practice. Unchanged transcriptions are given with quotation marks. The names of some well-known personages are given in English rather than in Navajo.

decided to follow it backward, and came to a hill and followed the track downward until he came to some dung, and in it there was fresh corn, and he was much surprised at finding this because it was the month of January. He followed on until he came to a little pool of water with grass growing around it, and he saw that there were many tracks coming to the water, one from the south, one from the east, and one from the west. The track that he was following was from the north.

(2) Suddenly four Coyotes came up out of the water and shook themselves on the edge of the pool, one standing at each of the cardinal points on the edge of the pool. "Nalth-keh-olth-eh" couldn't imagine where they came from, and he went close and looked down into the water, and when he did this he saw that the water was only as thick as paper, and that there was a ladder leading down through the water with four steps on it, and he went forward and began to go down the ladder. When he got to the bottom he found another country there, and walked off toward the east. He saw that it had rained a little and the country was covered with green grass, and that there was a pointed mountain there where some sunflowers were growing, and he walked onward toward the east where the country was fresh with rain and where lovely flowers of all kinds were covering the land. He came to a white house, with corn growing behind it. He looked off to the south and saw a blue house there, with blue corn growing behind it, and at the west there was a yellow house with yellow corn growing, and at the north a black house with black corn growing behind it; and it was all sweet corn.

(3) He knew that these were the houses of the Coyote people of the different colors, and so he went on and entered the white house at the east and found there a Coyote man and woman. The Coyote man said, "Where have you come from, my grandchild?" And the woman repeated the same phrase, and they both said, "We have never seen a human being here before." He stayed with them, and at sundown another person came in. He was a witch person *(yee naaldoshii)*, and he wore a Coyote skin over his back. The Coyote people asked "Nalth-keh-olth-eh" where he came from, and why he came, and he answered saying that on earth he had followed the Coyote tracks down to this place, and that he was hunting when he found the tracks. The Coyote people told him that he was the first of those living above who had ever come down, and they told him that when the people of the earth had pains in their legs, arms, back, or head, that these pains came from the bad Coyote people who lived in the lower world, and that the medicine to cure these pains was an offering made of pollen, turquoise, jet, white shell, and abalone, and the feathers of the canary,

bluebird, (female) eagle *('atsá tsa'ii)*, the beard of the turkey *(tazhii)*, and white cotton string, which should be put in four prayersticks colored white, blue, yellow, and black made of reed. They also told "Nalth-keh-olth-eh" that the noses of the good Coyotes were black because they had clouds on the ends of them, and their mouths were edged with all colors of the different flowers. They told him also that when the Coyotes howl they are calling up the rain, and that the colors on the flowers and on the ears of the Coyotes are made by the winds; white, blue, yellow, and black, and that the dark color on the top of the Coyotes' fur and on their tails is the rain, and the white color on their throats is the white dawn, while the yellow stripe on their legs is the yellow light of evening.

(4) The good Coyote people said, "If you want to learn our songs we will teach you," and "Nalth-keh-olth-eh" said he would like to learn, so they told him first about the prayersticks, then the prayers and the songs of the prayersticks, and how the sandpaintings should be made, and he stayed four nights learning these things. Then they told him to go up to the upper world and there to tell his brother and sisters what he had learned. When he was about to leave they brought four ears of the corn of four colors, and boiled this and gave it to him to eat. Then he left and went back to his home, after they had told him never to forget what he had learned, and they told him also that the water through which he passed to come down to their country should be used in the ceremony. They told him also that they had a *yé'ii*-god of their own, and a *haashch'ééłti'i* of their own, also two female *yé'ii*.[2]

(5) When "Nalth-keh-olth-eh" got home he began to teach his brother, who learned it all, and "Nalth-keh-olth-eh" held a nine-day ceremony over his brother using all the songs, prayersticks and sandpaintings, and "Nalth-keh-olth-eh" said that on the last night *(bitł'éé')* that the good Coyote people would come. When the last night came the Coyote people arrived, but they were wrapped in a fog so that they could not be seen, and they told "Nalth-keh-olth-eh" that he sang the songs well, and that the ceremony was good and that if he went on giving it as well as that, he would probably live to be very old, but if he did not do it well he would die very soon. (Medicine Man told me that he was sure these things are true because his father told him of it, and he thinks that he must have done well in his ceremonies because he has lived to be very old, and has been giving ceremonies since his father died twenty-four years ago.) This first ceremony was at "Tsenenni Koholtsi" near Mesa Verde.

---

[2]Probably should read, "...they had *yé'ii* gods of their own, a *haashch'ééłti'i* (Talking-god) and two female *yé'ii*."

(6) When it was finished *nítch'i biyáázh*, the Little Wind, came to "Nalth-keh-olth-eh" and said that there were two *hastói* (Holy People) living nearby, Talking-god and Calling-god, who had been making love to the two maidens who must never see the light *(doo bídeedláád)*, and that two babies had been born, and that the people of "Kinteel" (Hopis) were planning to kill these babies. "Nalth-keh-olth-eh" went to Talking-god and Calling-god and told them that this was going to happen, and "Nalth-keh-olth-eh" blew the sun down so that Talking-god and Calling-god could come in the darkness to where the babies were living, and the gods took them away with them. These babies were a white dog, son of Talking-god, and the yellow dog, the child of Calling-god.

(7) "Nalth-keh-olth-eh" then decided that he would like to go down to the lower world again to see if there was more that he could learn, and when he came into the white house where he had been before he found the same old Coyote man and woman living there, and they asked him what he wanted, and he said he wondered if there was anything more that he needed to learn about the ceremony, and he said, "You were present when I gave the Chant, was it all right?" They said, "You did it very well, but there is one more prayerstick that you must learn. This is the *iinéé'* (speaking) prayerstick. This is four inches long, painted half white and half yellow, and this medicine is for those who are crazy." So "Nalth-keh-olth-eh" learned the song and prayer that belonged to this prayerstick and he spent two nights with them, and when he was leaving they brought in again four ears of the corn of the four colors white, blue, yellow, and black, and he took this home with him, and when spring came he planted this corn.

(8) When it was ripe Coyote, the bad Coyote, and *hastói* stole into the corn at night and began to eat it. Coyote said, "It tastes good," but *hastói* said, "It tastes bitter to me." In the morning when "Nalth-keh-olth-eh" came into his field he saw that some people had been there stealing; he found some tracks in the arroyo nearby, and recognized those of Coyote and *hastói*, who when they saw "Nalth-keh-olth-eh" tracking them grew scared and began to run. Coyote ran faster because *hastói* had pains in his legs and could not run fast. So "Nalth-keh-olth-eh" and his family caught him and questioned him, asking why he had gone into the field and eaten the corn which was not ripe. *Hastói* said that Coyote had led him into this trouble, and so the people told *hastói* that the corn must not be stolen, and then they let him go. Later someone came to "Nalth-keh-olth-eh" asking for corn to plant when his seed was ripe, and "Nalth-keh-olth-eh" gave it to this person, who was *na'ashǫ'ii dich'izhii* (Horned Toad). He had planted it and when it was ripe in summer he built himself a brush hogan *(chaha'oh)* where he

lived, to watch the corn. One day Coyote came to visit him, and Horned Toad went to meet him and roasted some of the corn and gave it to Coyote who ate and said, "This tastes just like some of my own corn." Horned Toad said, "It is not your corn, it is mine." Coyote kept on saying, "It must be my corn," and every time Horned Toad said he was mistaken. Finally Coyote grew angry and threatened Horned Toad, and at last in a rage swallowed him, and then Coyote moved the brush hogan to a different place and went to live in it.

(9) Suddenly he heard a sound "sh" but he couldn't see anything, and said to himself, "No wonder I hear sounds for I am sitting in a *hok'ee hooghan* (house where someone has died)." So Coyote moved the hogan again, and when it was finished he laid down to sleep and this time he heard Horned Toad make a sound in his stomach. Coyote went round looking for Horned Toad but couldn't see anything, and being frightened he moved the hogan away for the third time, but as before he heard strange sounds, so he moved it for the fourth time, and went into the fields and brought in corn and ate it. Afterwards he heard the same sound again and this time he knew that it came from his stomach, and he said, "Is that you, Horned Toad?" and he answered, "Yes I am here."

(10) Horned Toad then asked Coyote what were the names of the different parts of his insides, and Coyote named them; intestines, stomach, etc. Horned Toad said first, "What are these two round things in here?" and Coyote answered, "They are my kidneys." Horned Toad asked, "What is this round red pointed thing?" and Coyote said, "It is my heart." Horned Toad said, "What are these two things near the red pointed thing which have a blue tube that runs into them?" Coyote said, "Those are my lungs, and that blue thing is my throat with which I swallowed you and my food." Then Horned Toad said, "I will cut your throat." Coyote begged for his life, but Horned Toad cut it and then came out backwards through Coyote's intestine.

(11) When Coyote had died, Horned Toad heard the call of Talking-god four times, and then he appeared and saw the Coyote dead, and that Horned Toad had killed him. Talking-god could not speak but made signs with his hands to show that as Coyote had been killed there would be no more rain or flowers, because he was the caller of the rain, but Horned Toad could not understand Talking-god.

(12) Then Little Wind appeared who was to be the messenger to be sent to Black Mountain to the Holy People living there, *tsé dah hastso* and *tó dootł'izh*, and Little Wind went to get the two Holy Ones in a mist invisibly, because they wanted these two Holy People to hold a ceremony and bring Coyote to life so that the rain and flowers could

come again to the earth. They came back with the messenger in a mist to the dead Coyote and brought two holy buckskins, and put these over and under the body, and then Talking-god walked over it back and forth, and Coyote came back to life and began to walk about and stretch himself. This is the reason buckskins are used in the ceremonies now, (in the *yé'iibicheii* etc.). When Coyote had recovered, Horned Toad said that the reason he had been killed was because he had claimed that the corn belonging to Horned Toad was his, and the reason that he had been brought back to life was because he was the caller of the rain.

(13) Then Coyote went off and came to a place where *na'ashǫ'ii łibáii* (Lizards) were sliding down the rocks. Coyote wanted to try sliding with them, but the Lizards said that he must not. Coyote paid no attention to them but went up high on the rocks and began to slide, but he went sideways and a rock fell on him and nearly squashed him, but he recovered from this without any help and went on his way.

(14) Then he came to where *dahsání* (Porcupine) was living and Coyote went into his house. The Porcupine began to eat bark off of the piñon tree and scratched his nose and it bled and the blood ran over the bark of the piñon, and as it did so the bark changed into dried meat and he put it on the fire to roast it for Coyote, and he ate it and said that it tasted very good. Then he invited Porcupine to come and visit him, and when later he came Coyote tried to feed him in the same way, but only managed to burn his nose and the bark and none could eat it.

(15) Later Coyote came to the home of *nahashch'id* (the Badger), and to entertain him, Badger took some rotten old soapweed and spat on it and put it on the fire to cook, and when he took it off the fire it had turned into two prairie dogs which tasted very good. Coyote asked Badger to visit him later and when Badger came Coyote tried to feed him on cooked soapweed and spat on it, but all that happened was that the ashes flew up in his eyes, and there was no food.

(16) Then Coyote went on and came to the house of *ayałchi'í*, the Red Winged Blackbird, who spread his wings to receive Coyote and as he did so the whole place turned red. Coyote asked the Blackbird how he did this, and the bird said that he had fires hidden around the room which he could light with his wings. Then Coyote asked the Blackbird to visit him, and later when he came, Coyote had placed fires around his room and he blew on them, but the fires did not turn red and there was no light.

(17) Then Coyote went on his way and met a Doe and her young ones which he admired very much and asked the Doe how she made

their pretty spots. The Doe said that she put her young ones in the cracks of the rocks and then built a fire nearby and the sparks flew on them and that was what made their spots. Afterwards Coyote went home to try and make his young ones as pretty as the little Deer. So he put them in a crack of the rocks and built a fire close to them, and the young Coyotes began to cry but he told them to stop because he was only trying to make them pretty as the Deer. When the big fire had died out he found his young ones were all roasted, and their lips were brown and drawn up off their teeth. He laid them out side by side thinking that they were smiling at him because he could see their teeth, and he talked to them but they didn't answer and he knew that they were dead, and so he went on his travels.

(18) He next came to some birds who were making arrows; they were *ch'íshii sháshii* (Titmice). They were making the arrows of pine and spruce and Coyote said to them, "You couldn't kill anything with those arrows," but they said, "Let us try our arrows on you." Then they blew the arrows at him while he dodged about, but the arrows followed him and he hid away in a hole in a rock, but the magic arrows followed him even there and hit him and entered his body under the tail and killed him.

(19) Later on he came back to life and went back to his home where he had two female children still living. He felt very sick and said that he was going to die, and told his daughters that when he was dead to put him up on the roof, and that when they saw flies gathering around they would know that he was dead, and then that they were to leave him there and go away to live. So when they thought he had died they did what he said and put him up on the roof and left him there. He had with him some cedar berries hidden away, and he began firing off these berries which made a sound like flies buzzing and his daughters moved away to a distance across a hill and settled down there when they were sure that their father had died. Coyote had told his daughters that if they ever met a man carrying a bow and arrows and a lion skin quiver that he would be a good man for them to marry, as he was a friend of his. After the girls had been living at their new home for some time Coyote climbed down off the roof and dressed himself as the man he had described to the girls, with bow and arrows, and his face painted with *ch'ídootł'izh* (a blue stripe below the eyes). He came up to the two girls and asked them whence they came from and where their brothers lived, and they told him that their brothers were dead. Coyote said that he had come to visit their brothers and have a good time with them and he asked the girls what they had said before they died, because they were so clever and told so many stories (there was

a song about this), and he pretended to cry about their death. The girls said that their brothers had said nothing, but they said, "Our father told us before he died to marry a man who should come to us with a blue painted face and carrying bows and arrows and a lion skin quiver." Coyote said, "I was sure that my brother said something before he died, he was so intelligent." Then Coyote told them to come with him, and they went on to where a tree grew, and built a brush hogan there and spent the night together. When the morning came they built a fire and Coyote asked the girls to look for lice on his head, and lay down to sleep with his head on the lap of one of the girls. While he slept they saw a wart on his neck that was like their father's, and the youngest girl recognized him and spoke to her sister about it. Then Coyote woke up and heard the girls talking and said, "Yes, I am your father," and he ran off and left them crying.

(20) He went on to where some people were living and as he came near they called out to him, "You are the man that has married his daughters," and he fled and went on. Then he came to another home and went in and the people said again, "That is the man that married his daughters," and he fled away. He came to a third house and the same thing happened again and he fled on. Then he went up on a hill and said to himself, "It must be the Wind, Little Wind, that tells the people what I have done," and he lifted up his tail and caught the Wind there and let it pass into his body.

(21) Then he went on and came to a place where a woman was living who had twelve brothers that were all hunters. She was rich, had lots of meat, and was working on buckskins, sewing them together. Coyote asked her where the rest of her family was. She said, "All the rest of my family have been killed by a Giant (*yé'iitsoh*) and I will marry anyone who will kill that Giant." She was boiling some meat with the bones and gave some to Coyote and he ate it, but hid one of the bones in his clothes and then went on, carrying the meat with him. He came to the home of the Giant and Coyote asked him if he would like to be a good runner, and that if so he would make him swift but that they must both take a sweat bath before the ceremony. (Coyote had with him the bone and two stones and a knife.) So they made ready the sweat bath and the Giant went in first, and Coyote asked him if he was hot enough. He said, "Yes," and then Coyote began to massage him. The Giant said, "Perhaps I had better rub you first," and Coyote said, "All right," and gave the knife and the two rocks to the Giant. The Giant meant to kill Coyote and began by trying to cut his thigh with the knife, but he had laid the bone on it and the Giant was fooled and thought he had already cut the flesh off Coyote's

thigh. Then the Giant tried to break the bone, thinking it was Coyote's thigh, with the two rocks that he held, but after he had hammered it hard and broken it Coyote moved the bone away, and when the Giant felt for it he touched Coyote's leg which was whole and unhurt and Coyote spat on his leg and told the Giant that in this way the leg was healed. Then he told the Giant that it was his turn, and the Giant gave back the knife and rocks to Coyote who had previously hidden his bone in the dark of the sweat bath. Then Coyote cut the Giant's thigh to the bone and broke it with the two rocks, one held below and one above as a hammer. The Giant cried when his leg was broken and said he was killed, and Coyote ran off taking the Giant's clothes and his game bag and brought them to the woman's house and left them outside the door. Then he went in and said, "You promised you would marry anyone who would kill the Giant. Go outside and see what is there." So the woman went out, and it was now sundown and she saw the Giant's clothing there. Then she came in again, and by now it was dark, and she made their bed and they slept together.

(22) Next morning the brothers came back bringing much meat with them, and Coyote saw them coming and hid himself behind the bedding. They came in and built a fire and after they had done this they smelt something, but they couldn't make out what it was. Then they built the fire higher but still were conscious that someone was in their home. They kept putting more wood on the fire, but, though they still smelled the stranger, they could not find him. Four times they did this, and finally Coyote was so hot that he jumped out from behind the bed, and he told the brothers that he had married their sister. They were not pleased and went outdoors and built a fire at a little distance and said, "Let the married people stay in there," and the brothers cooked their food outside on this fire and stayed there. Later the woman came out and went to her brothers and said that Coyote, her husband, wanted to go hunting with them, but they refused saying they did not want him, and she went back and she told this to Coyote. Then the woman went out again and begged her brothers to take Coyote with them, but they said he always made mischief and they did not want him. The woman asked her brothers the same question four times, and finally they agreed to take Coyote with them to their hunting in *tséyi'* Canyon. They started their hunt by crossing the canyon on a rainbow, and they warned Coyote to keep his eyes shut and then they all sat down on the rainbow taking Coyote between them. He would not keep his eyes entirely closed and peeped out through his eyelids, and as he did this the rainbow began to sink, and the hunters said, "You must keep your eyes shut." This frightened him, and they landed safely on the other side.

(23) Coyote suggested that he should chase the mountain sheep towards the hunters while they stayed near the canyon. Then he shredded some bark of cedar trees and tied this to his tail and ran off up the mountains, and they heard him calling, and they saw smoke and knew that he had been firing the brush to chase out the game, and finally saw him running towards them chasing some sheep. The hunters were ready for them and killed many sheep and began to butcher them and Coyote said he wanted the horns as his portion. In those days of long ago the mountain sheep horns were made of fat, and he wanted to eat the horns. The hunters agreed to give him this portion but Coyote did not believe them, and he was so suspicious and angry because he was afraid they were going to take the horns, that he said, "I wish the horns would turn into solid bone and then you will get no food from them." And when the hunters came to cut the horns they found that they were so hard that they could not do it. The hunters were angry and said, "This is what we knew he would do, he always makes mischief. That is the reason we did not want him." When the meat was all cut up they packed it into a small bundle and gave it to Coyote to carry home. They told him that he should go along the rim of the canyon and that he must not look off into the canyon or lay the bundle down until he reached home. Coyote said, "That is easy, the bundle is light, I can carry it," and ran off with it.

(24) Very soon he disobeyed what he had been told and laid the bundle down and went to the edge of the canyon to look off. There he saw some people playing gambling games below, and Coyote called to them jeeringly, "I have got the woman that you wanted," and he called them rude names such as fuzzy hair. When he got tired of talking to the people he went back to where he had left the meat, but he found the bundle broken and the meat scattered and he could not manage to tie it into such a small bundle again, though he pounded it well. The people who were in the canyon were very angry at Coyote's words to them and sent *na'ashjé'ii hastiin* the Spiderman, to go after Coyote and punish him. Spiderman climbed up to the rim of the canyon on his rope, unseen by Coyote, and Spiderman caught him and wound him up in his rope. Then the people of the canyon, *chaa'* (Beaver), *tábąąstíín* (Otter), and *táshchozhii* (Water Swallows) came up to the top of the canyon and Coyote was frightened when he saw them and tried to run away, but each time that he tried the Spiderman's rope brought him up short, and then all the canyon people gathered around him and carried him down into the canyon. He was still carrying a little bundle of the meat but left a good deal of it on the top of the canyon. The people carried him to their home where they had been playing "Nah-hah-jonsh" which is played with hoops and a

pole, and Coyote asked if he could play it with them, and they agreed to this and he bet the meat that he was carrying but lost it all in play. Then he bet his own fur and his arrow pouch made of lion-skin. He knew that the water animals often bet their fur because if they lost it they could go into the water and get more fur, and he thought he could do this too. So he went on playing and lost his bet, and his fur and his arrow pouch, and all the people began pulling his fur off beginning at the tail, and they had a hard time pulling it off his tough nose. After he had lost his fur he jumped into the water but came out naked as when he went into it, and four times he jumped into the water hoping to get his fur back, but his eyes swelled and he was very miserable, so the people decided to put him in Badger's hole to keep warm. Coyote's fur was cut up in small pieces and all the water animals took these pieces and tied them on their necks and stomachs and different places, and that is why these animals have white patches on their bodies. Some of the birds took his fur also and that gave them their white markings.

(25) The hunters meanwhile went home and before they went into the house broke some branches off of piñon and cedar and brought them into the hogan and built a fire. The woman asked her brothers what had become of her husband and they said that he had left them long ago to go home, but the woman thought that her brothers had killed him. The hunters said he must have looked down into the canyon as he went along and have seen the canyon people gambling and have joined them. The woman decided to go and see the gamblers and find out whether her husband was there. But before she started she took out her heart and left it behind.

(26) When she arrived at the home of the gamblers they began shooting at her and drove her away, so she went home again, badly wounded, for there were arrows sticking in her body. And she also brought in piñon and cedar branches and built a fire with them. Then she began walking around the fire, singing as she went, and as she did this the arrows dropped out of her body, and she was well. She went back for the second time to the gamblers' home and again they shot her and chased her away wounded, and as before when she came home she brought in cedar and piñon and made a fire and walked around it singing, and the arrows came out of her body and she was healed. By now her arms were beginning to be hairy below the elbows and her nose was growing longer, and her teeth were growing long and like those of a bear. She went again for the third time to the gamblers' place and everything happened as before, and by now she had become hairy as far as her shoulders, and her teeth and nose were just like those of a bear. Then for the fourth time she went out to find her husband

and went to the gamblers' home, and this time she saw her husband, for he didn't die when he was put into the Badger's hole. The woman who now was called *shash náádleehí* (Changing Bear Woman) told her husband that he was to go back to his own people at *tsé dah hastso* and at *tó dootł'izh*, and so Coyote went off down the canyon to join his people. Since this last adventure he has always been, as he is now, the color of a badger, but originally he was many colored and beautiful. Coyote was not the person who brought the *mą'iijí hatáál* to men. Changing Bear Woman went back to her home wounded as the gamblers had shot at her again, built her fire, and walked around it as before, singing, and as she did this she became a bear.

(27) All this time her brothers were away, except the youngest brother who had seen her turning into a bear and hid himself under a flat rock in the floor, for he was terrified of her. The place where she had hidden her heart was under an oak tree outside the house, and Chipmunk *(hazéísts'ósii)* was the only one who knew where it was buried. The Bear Woman knew that her youngest brother was somewhere inside the house, and began digging around until she found the rock and her brother. She pretended to be kind and said, "My poor brother, is that where you are?" But the Little Wind was advising the young brother how to save his life, and fortunately the young brother had his bow and arrows with him. Then the Bear Woman said, "Let me comb your hair for you." By now it was afternoon and the Little Wind told Younger Brother to sit where he could see his shadow and hers as she did his hair. So he sat down outside, and the Bear Woman began to comb his hair and he watched her shadow, and when he saw her open her mouth over him he would move aside, and all the time he held his bow and arrows. The Chipmunk also had told the boy where the Bear Woman's heart was buried, and he said to the boy, "Watch me and where I jump up and down that will be the place where the heart is buried." So after the Bear Woman had combed his hair for a time the boy jumped up, got out his bow and arrows and ran off to the place where the Chipmunk was jumping about, and when he came to the place he could see the heart beating under the earth. The Bear Woman ran after him but before she caught him the boy shot his arrow into the buried heart and the blood began to run out of it, and the Bear Woman fell dead. The heart's blood began to flow also and the two streams of blood ran towards each other, and the Little Wind told the boy not to let the streams join, for if they did the Bear Woman would come to life again.

(28) So the Bear Woman died and the boy cut her up beginning between her legs and he threw this part under the large soapweed and

it changed into *hashk'aan* (wild bananas). He then cut off her breasts and threw them into a piñon tree and they turned into piñon and cedar berries. Then he cut off her head and threw it into a tree and this turned into a prickly pine, and he threw her feet away and they changed into badgers. Every time he threw part of her body away he said "We will make use of this in the future," and as we all know the Bear's and Badger's hands look much like those of human beings. Then the boy cut her body open and took out her guts and they changed into birds. Then the Chipmunk dipped his paws in blood and striped his back with it, and the Gopher marked her face with the blood.

Coyoteway Myth of William Charlie

This myth was recorded by Maud Oakes in 1942 or 1943. The manuscript has been kept at the Museum of Navaho Ceremonial Art in Santa Fe. Permission to print was obtained from Maud Oakes—graciously mediated by Caroline Olin and Bertha Dutton.

The informant, William Charlie, lived near Smith Lake. He is a member of the "Sour Water" (Bitter Water) clan. His version of Coyoteway he learned from his father, "Cai Hi Edge," a member of the Forest clan. William was one of twin singers. Five sandpaintings, given in the subsequent pages, belong to this ceremonial.

This Coyoteway myth is ethnologically very important; it is the only evidence we have of an Evilway version of Coyoteway. The myth, together with the extant sandpaintings, suggests an origin closer to the Navajo-Apachean hunter stratum than do the remaining available Coyoteway materials.

Paragraph (1) refers to "emergence" mythology only in passing. More important is the young hunter's relationship with Deer-raiser, the traditional Apachean "Master of Animals." In the same manner in which the shamanic hero of the Plumeway tradition has found Deer-raiser's home—by the method of using pointers—so the hero of this Coyoteway myth, leaving the realm of Deer-raiser, finds the home of Coyote Man, another hunter. The empowering experience of this first Coyoteway shaman takes place in the traditional geography of hunters. Young Man learns from Coyote Man in the Surface World;

he does not yet seek power from below the Pueblo Indian central hole of emergence.

The frenzied performance of Coyote Man in paragraph (2) results in the downing of the Black Thunder Bird. Coyote Man, a hunter, obtains his healing power in the same manner in which he hunts—by trickery.

As paragraphs (3) through (7) reveal, the first human shaman, Young Man, learns by watching his tutelary, the masterful Coyote Man. Elsewhere in Apachean mythology the visits of shamanic heroes at the home of Deer-raiser serve the hunter's purpose of obtaining game animals. In the present myth the hunter shaman switches his interests to obtaining healing power. For that reason he leaves the realm of Deer-raiser and enters the realm of a fellow hunter. Deer-raiser, in ancient hunter traditions, has been a game animal elder. Coyote, on the other hand, is a fellow hunter; he is a tutelary who has so advanced the hunter's art of trickery that he and his apprentices can safely venture into the territory of the more powerful gods. Healing power is obtained in the course of his daring.

Paragraphs (8) through (10) have nothing to do with the origin of the Coyoteway Evilway ceremonial. At most, this "appendix" demonstrates the shaman's ability in trickery—his Coyote power. Gambling is a form of conventionalized trickery. The episodes narrated here do not depict Pueblo culture as it actually functioned when the first Apacheans began roaming in the Southwest; rather, they illustrate remarkably well how the Apachean hunters felt toward the Pueblo Indians.

(1) The story starts at Blue House, where they first came up to this world.[1] There were two places, one in the west and one in the east. At *tó hwiidzoh*, the place of Deer-raiser, lived a young man. His grandfather and grandmother were First Man and First Woman. He started from the western place, traveling on top of the red mesa, till he came to a place called *waa'*, or Bee-weed. He was traveling in an easterly direction. At this time people were living all over the place, especially at Pueblo Bonito. They were cliff dwellers and great gamblers. Young Man did not want to go to these places as he was hunting deer and other game. When he arrived at Bee-weed he saw a fire at Mountain-by-itself. He saw it four nights, and during the day he looked for the place of the light. The fourth night he wanted to be sure, so he pointed

---

[1]Wherever possible, the Navajo transcriptions of the original author have been brought into conformity with current practice. Unchanged transcriptions are given with quotation marks. The names of some well-known personages are given in English rather than in Navajo.

two sticks at it. The next morning he went to the place, the direction the two sticks pointed to, and he found a hogan. It was the home of the Coyotes. Inside he found a Coyote man who was "Ma-i-nao-il," or Coyote-out-of-mind, or Coyote-who-changes-around. He wore skins of all colors. That he wore. Some were even of mixed colors. When the Coyote man saw (the young man) he said, "What are you doing in my house? This is no place for a human being." "I am looking for deer and game and something to eat," (the young man) said. Coyote Man said, "I am a hunter, I live here and hunt all the time. There is a place where I always go hunting, called Bunch-of-sheep. There are people there who get angry with me and I fight with them. That is why some of my skin is scorched. They are called Lightning People." After he had said all this, the Coyote man thought (by himself), this is a good man and he should know something besides hunting. I shall put into this man what I know, so that he and his children can have my wisdom and everything they want. He said to the young man, "Come with me to Bunch-of-sheep Place, and just watch me from a distance. Watch what I do." Before they left Coyote Man started a song, and this is where the first Coyote song belongs.

(2) They started, but before they arrived it began to cloud over, and when they were near it began to rain. Coyote Man said to the young man, "Wait here." He then turned clockwise and then counter-clockwise. The Lightning tried to hit him, but he would swing, first one way and then another, and the Lightning would miss him. This made a lot of dust and went on for an hour. When it was all over he returned to the young man who then saw that Coyote Man had streaks on his body burnt deep enough to draw blood. He was also covered with mud.

(3) Coyote Man said, "Now my grandson you have seen what I have done. You have seen how angry the Lightning People are. They have no mercy, but I have no fear of them." After this they returned to the Coyote man's hogan and lay down inside. "Dontso" came around with his bundle and in it he had buckskin and turquoise. He told Coyote Man that the Black Thunder Bird had fallen on the ground and was paralyzed. "Dontso" piled the buckskins and turquoise in front of Coyote Man and asked him to cure the Thunder Bird. Coyote Man said, "That is not enough." "Dontso" put many more skins in front of him on the ground, but still, Coyote Man wanted more. "Dontso" said, "I shall send messages to the Holy People, for if Thunder Bird stays on the ground everything will go wrong on earth." "Dontso" sent word to Canyon de Chelly, near *dibé ntsaa* and to "Sa-id-ah," Edge of Canyon, also to Talking-god and the Lightning People. His message was that Coyote Man would not make medicine. "Dontso" sent this message by the Sun's rays.

(4) The Holy People came to the place where Coyote Man was, and they talked of the Thunder Bird who had fallen on the ground. The Lightning People said, "We know what to do to make him well. We have all herbs, the prayers, the songs and everything that goes with the Coyote Chant. The Black Thunder Bird is Black Lightning, our head man. We shall give all these things to the Coyote Man so that he will make our head man well. What we will give him will be much more useful to him than the piles of buckskins on the ground." So "Dontso" went to see the Black Lightning Man and told him what had been decided. "It is good," said Black Lightning Man, "I will give everything as I do not want to be paralyzed like this." "Dontso" returned and told Coyote Man what Black Lightning had said. "I am happy now to make him well," said Coyote Man. But he did not believe that the Lightning Man would give him the prayers and the songs, and he asked four times whether the songs and prayers were holy or just made up.

(5) They started off for Lightning Man, and when they arrived they found him lying on the ground. Coyote Man made four lightnings in each of the four directions around the body of the Lightning Man,

then he stepped over him four times. Lightning Man sat up. Coyote Man asked him whether it was true that he would give all. He asked him this four times. Then Coyote Man said, "From now on I shall be chief of all rains and over the weather. Though you will live in the sky where the water is, you will sometimes get thirsty. From now on don't fight with me!" After he had made the Lightning Man well, Coyote Man asked about the songs and prayers. He was then taught all the songs and the prayers, and the herbs and how to use them. Lightning Man said, "In the future all these things which I have taught you will be useful." The young man had been watching everything that had taken place. Coyote Man said, "I will put in some of what I know and add it to your chant, and it will be called 'Coyote Chant, the Evil

Way.' The offerings and the prayersticks with the Fire Pit Ritual will be done on the first four days, the dry-paintings will start on the fifth day. All the prayersticks and the jewels are for the Holy People. When the offerings are given the Holy People come and get them."

(6) They made the prayersticks, they offered these together with the jewels, and in the evening they made a white cornmeal painting. This painting is made in the evenings of the first and second days. After

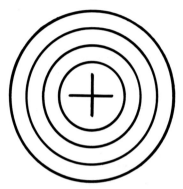

walking on to it from the east, the patient sits in the middle. As the patient sits in the center he smokes wild tobacco in a pipe. Then everyone else smokes. Medicine is put on the patient's eyes and ears so that he can see and hear (the) evil. Medicine comes from prayerstick powder, the dirt in a badger's ear, and from the water in the watery part of a live eagle's eye. Small pieces of a poisonous herb are ground up and eaten by the singer and the patient. These herbs can then never harm them. Then they speak the Talking-god Prayer.

(7) Coyote Man said, "In the future when a man goes insane, or if he is bitten by a coyote or a mad dog, if he misbehaves sexually, or if he does not want to work and do anything because he is scared, these paintings will be done for him, the prayers and songs will be done over him. This will also be useful for men who go hunting."

(8) It took four days to learn all the prayers, songs, and paintings. The Young Man, the hunter, had watched all this and then said to them, "Thank you, I have learned it also. Now I shall go my way." He left and arrived at a place near Crown Point called "Heart Rock." The people at Pueblo Bonito were gambling and doing much evil. So the Young Man sent word of this to Big Snake at Mount Taylor, and also to the place called "Rocks Pointing Skyward," as well as to the Bat People. The Bats and Snakes came to the Young Man and they talked about all the evil that was being done, they decided to put an end to it all. They started out for Pueblo Bonito. Before they started they wanted to gamble so that they could beat the gamblers at their own

game. So they had a hoop game. Snake Man was the hoop. They had a ball game, and Weasel was the ball. They had a stick game, and the Bat threw the sticks in the air. The Wind People also wanted to take part in the games.

(9) Before they arrived at Canyon de Chelly the young hunter said, "Wait here, I want to see what they are doing." So he went ahead and came to a well where he met the chief gambler's wife. The chief had slaves working for him. The Young Man asked the wife whether her husband was at home. The young deer hunter looked so much like a gambler that the wife thought he was her husband. She went to her house in the pueblo, and the Young Man went also. The wife went into her house, and the Young Man followed her. She said to her husband whom she found in the house, "How did you return so quickly?" Then the Young Man entered the house and the gambler said, "Every day people come to gamble with me. No one has ever defeated me. Have you come to gamble with me?" The Young Man said, "No, you are my brother." "I have never seen you before, I don't know you, let's gamble," said the Gambler. He took the gambling sticks. The Young Man wanted to gamble the buckskins he had, so they both made piles of buckskins.

(10) The Young Man, the hunter, threw the sticks and won. The Gambler was angry and said, "You have cheated me." The Gambler's bet this time was some girls. Young Man put up as his bet the Bat. The Young Man threw the sticks and won again. The Bat had helped him by catching the sticks in the air and by throwing them back quickly. The Gambler said, "Let's try another game, one with hoops." The Gambler said, "We will use my hoop." The Young Man said, "You use your hoop and I shall use my own." They went out on a flat ground. The Big-snake Man was Young Man's hoop. Big Snake said, "Whatever you do, don't hit me hard with your stick." For the hoops were to be rolled with sticks. Young Man said to the Gambler, "I will bet all that I have won from you." The Gambler bet his slaves. The Young Man won again. The Gambler said, "Let's play ball." There was a big hole in a rock, whoever could bat the ball into the hole won. The Gambler batted first. He had bet all his jewelry. He hit the ball at the hole and Wind blew it away. He missed each time. The Young Man, the hunter, took his weasel ball and the Wind blew it into the hole. He won again. The Gambler said, "Let's run a race." He bet everything he had in the world, and Young Man bet all he had won. The Weasel made holes under the track where the Gambler would run. Young Man and the Gambler ran their race. The Young Man won as the Gambler fell and lost. After he had lost he wanted to try something else. He dug a hole three feet deep and put a log into it. It was to test their strength. Who-

ever broke it off would win. The Young Man, the hunter, told the Worm to go into it. The Gambler had gambled the whole pueblo. The Young Man went first and broke it off. The Gambler had lost all and therefore said to one of his men, "I have lost all, go and kill him with the stone axe that I have thrown on the ground." The slave hit himself instead and killed himself, and so did the others also. The Gambler said to the hunter, "Hit yourself on the head with this axe." The hunter, the Young Man, said, "No, this is enough," and took the axe from the Gambler. The hunter took a black bow, and the Gambler stood on it. The hunter said, "We will not kill you but send you away so you won't return. The Gambler was shot up into the Sky World by the bow. They heard him say something as he went but could not understand what he said. All the people came together and the hunter, the Young Man, told them to go home, that there was nothing to worry about anymore. They must go back to their work, to their crops. The hunter went back to the river where he had his home, to the mountain called *tó hwiidzoh*, the Place of Deer-raiser.

Sandpainting Reproductions

On file in the Museum of Navaho Ceremonial Art (now Wheelwright Museum), at Santa Fe, are twelve Coyoteway sandpainting reproductions (Packet 14). During the years from 1928 through 1946 these were collected by members and friends of the Museum from three different Coyoteway singers. The explanations which accompany the sandpainting designs are sketchy and may not be reliable at every point; nevertheless, they contain many helpful suggestions. With permission and by the courtesy of the Museum of Navaho Ceremonial Art I shall include here the available information, to complete the record.

Sandpaintings by Big Mustache

This group of early Coyoteway sandpaintings, of the years 1928 and 1929, is of greatest interest for the present study. The informant "Ta Cathlain" (Big Mustache) is very likely the same as *bidaghaa' łani* (Many Whiskers), the grandfather and teacher of our Man With Palomino Horse.

[224]

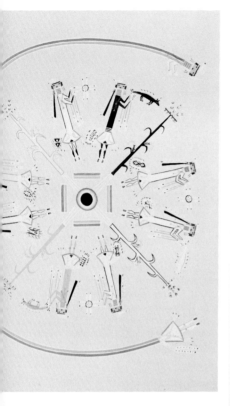

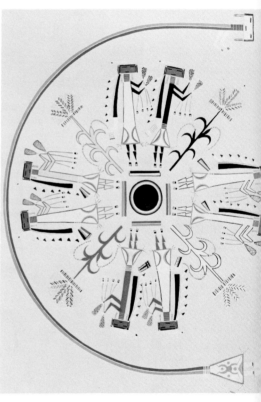

1. This sandpainting is the second in the chant;[1] it has, therefore, half the number of animals and plants. The top of this design is north. Collected by Laura Armer at Black Mountain in 1928. Repainted by Mrs. F.J. Newcomb.

2. The figures are Coyote Girls carrying sweet corn. The central water is the "old house of Coyote." Coyote is Navajo. He has power to bring rain and snow. Drought comes from killing coyotes. The black and white bar under the feet of the figures in the north (top of the design) is "rain in the distance." Collected at Black Mountain in 1929 and repainted by Laura Armer.

[1]References to ceremonial sequence are somewhat confusing in these notes. The reason for this might be that some sandpaintings were sketched during different performances and filed on separate occasions.

3. Coyote Girls carrying sweet corn. The Girls in four colors are flanked by corn plants of the same color. The center has a crossed rainbow. The top of this design is north. Collected by Laura Armer.

4. This sandpainting is the second in the Coyote Chant.[1] It depicts sunrays and sunset, Coyote Girls and foxes, and between them coyotes walking home. Seen under their feet are the rainbow in the east, sunray in the south, sundogs in the west, and black and white rain in the north. The little animals with feathers are foxes. Eight stalks of corn are growing out of the central water. The top of this design is north. Collected at Black Mountain in 1928 (1929?) and repainted by Laura Armer.

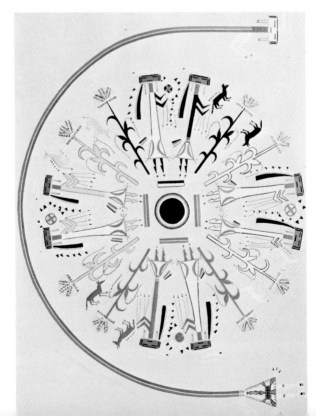

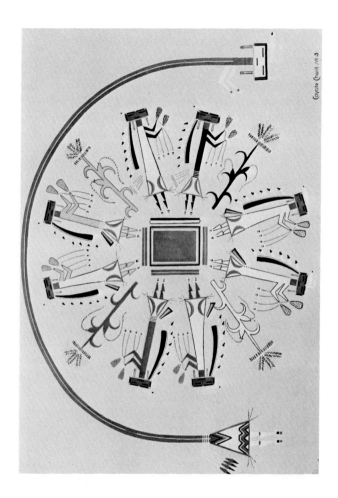

5. This sandpainting is the third.[1] It is similar to the first except for the rectangular central water (a home symbol?).[2] In all pictures the plants are corn. There are here no baskets. The top of this design is north. Coyote Girls are shown with corn ears in their hands. Four stalks of corn are growing out of the central water, which is blue (a home symbol). Collected at Black Mountain in 1929 and repainted by Laura Armer.

[2]In accordance with Coyoteway mythology, blue water is simply the entrance way to the underworld home of the divine Coyote People. It is not a general symbol of "home." Neither is the rectangle a specific symbol of the home. It is simply a way of stylizing the central water hole in accordance with the four cardinal directions.

Sandpaintings and Prayersticks by Bit'ahnii Bidághaaí

A set of two entirely different Coyoteway sandpaintings was obtained in 1938 from a certain *bit'ahnii bidághaaí*. These reproductions are significant because they show that Coyoteway has been performed with different kinds of sandpaintings—thus also in accordance with different kinds of theories or mythological traditions. The first sandpainting seems to support the claim of some informants, that Coyoteway belongs together with the so-called Excessway. Butterflies and Coyote both figure in "Excessway" mythology (see Haile 1978, and Luckert 1978). The prayersticks described by *bit'ahnii bidághaaí* likewise suggest a different version of Coyoteway.

1. This is the first sandpainting of the Coyote Chant. It shows the homes of the different coyotes: white dawn, blue sky, black night, and yellow evening. Four butterflies are on the path of pollen leading to the central spring of water. The function of the Coyote is to call up the rain. The top of this painting appears to be north. Repainted by Pierre Woodmann, after notes by Wheelwright and William P. Henderson, of November 20, 1938.

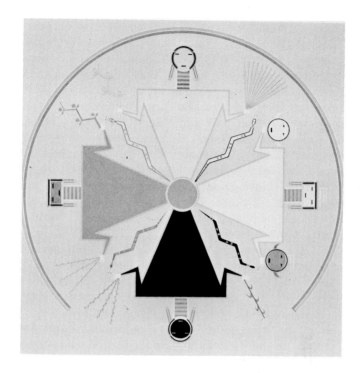

2. This sandpainting represents the four different Holy Times of Day, arranged around the central water. They hold corn, squash, beans, reeds and medicine in their hands. The eastern figure of Dawn holds the Sun and the Moon in her hands. Racer snakes are between the figures of the Holy Times of Day. The opening in the rainbow is in the south, not in the usual east. Repainted by Pierre Woodmann after notes by Wheelwright and William P. Henderson.

3. Not shown—drawings of prayersticks. On the second day six prayersticks are made. All are painted in solid colors. A blue prayerstick is made for Sky, a white one for Earth; then a blue, a black, a yellow, and a white prayerstick are made for the coyotes. On the third day ten prayersticks are made in the following sequence: white, yellow, brown, blue, black, red, white, brown, blue, black. They are for the ten chiefs of the coyotes.

Sandpaintings by William Charlie

Another set of sandpaintings, of 1946, comes from William Charlie of the "Sour Water" (Bitter Water) clan. He learned from his father, "Cai Hi-Edge," a Forest clansman. William was one of twin singers. These specimens demonstrate not only that various types of sandpaintings could exist in different versions of the Coyoteway ceremonial, but that they could be varied within each ceremonial in accordance with the singer's aims. So, for example, hunting and healing require different designs. It seems possible that hunting has been the older of these two concerns in Coyote-oriented ceremonialism. But then, since Holyway type offenses against Holy People happen most easily during hunting, the concerns of sickness and health are closely linked with it. It is possible that most among the older Navajo healing ceremonials have come into being as extensions of hunting rites.

Additional questions are raised about these sandpaintings by the copresence of a Coyoteway myth by William Charlie, an Evilway version printed in Chapter 11. What exactly constituted the Coyoteway ceremonial of William Charlie? What is the relationship between Holyway type and Evilway versions of Coyoteway? What is their relationship to the traditional ways of hunting? Quite obviously, these questions can not be dealt with in the limited scope of this book.

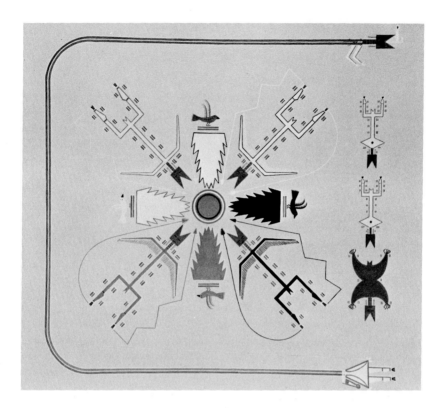

1. This ceremony is given for insane people, and for those bitten by a mad dog or coyote—also for sexual misbehavior and for hunting. It is a nine-night ceremony, and the prayersticks and offerings are given during the first four days. In the sandpainting of the fifth day the center is black water, outlined by "water pollen" of the four colors: white, blue, yellow, and red. The gods presented here are Thunder Birds. On their heads are flint caps. From their feet come male and female lightning arrows. The black bird and black clouds are to the east. The red feathered bird and white fog are to the north. Yellow birds and yellow clouds are to the west. Blue bird and blue fog are to the south. In the entrance to the east are Bat, Big Fly Messenger, and Yellow Bird Messenger. The sandpainting is encircled by Rainbow God wearing a flint hat. First to fifth day (series).[3] This sandpainting (and assumedly all the numbers which follow in this section) was collected in 1946 by Maud Oakes and was repainted by H. D. Ross.

2. Not shown—a sandpainting given on the sixth day. It is identical with the preceding sandpainting, with only a change in the color of the water.

---

[3]The numbering of the days, as it applies to William Charlie's sandpaintings, is somewhat confusing. This may be so because singers of nine-night ceremonials occasionally divide them into two halves and start counting the fifth night (the first of the second half) again as number one. Since prayerstick offerings were indeed given during the first four days, one might suspect that also in this version of Coyoteway all sandpaintings were made during the second half of the nine-night sequence. In this case it would seem possible, that sandpainting number one was for the fifth and number two for the sixth day as stated, that number three was for the seventh (?) or eighth day, number four for the eighth day, and number five for the seventh or eighth day of the nine-night sequence. At the same time, it is also possible that Coyoteway, for the purpose of hunting, has been a shorter ceremony than the full nine-night version.

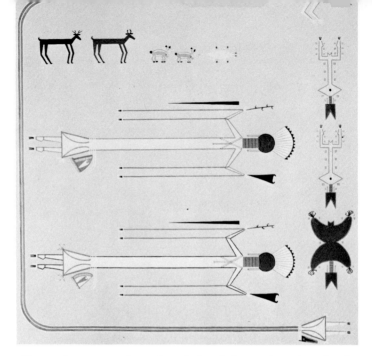

3. This sandpainting can be used on the fourth day in place of number five. It is more apt to be used if the patient is going to hunt. It is made after the steam bath. The gods and animals are the same as in number five. The top is north. First through fifth day (series).

4. This sandpainting (like number three) can be used on the fourth day in place of number five. It is more apt to be used if the patient is going to hunt. It is made after the steam bath. The gods and the animals are the same as in number five. The top is north. First to fifth day (series).

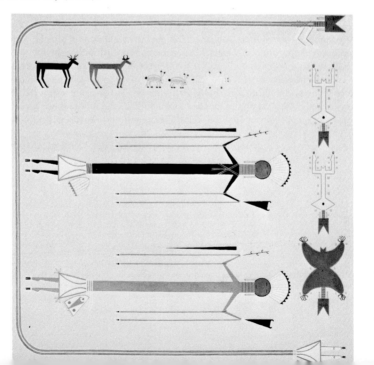

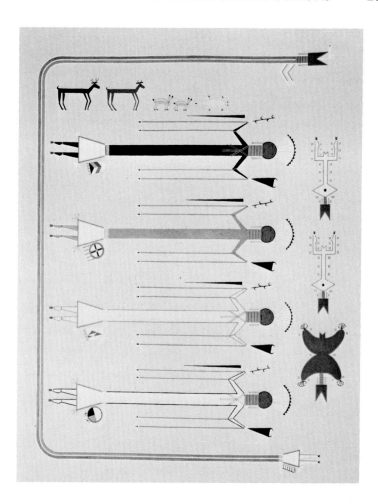

5. This sandpainting is given on the third or fourth day. The figures are Black Talking-god—yellow the same, and Blue Talking-god—white the same.[4] In the right hands of the gods are different plants. Below their right hands are hunting canes. In their left hands are the heads of deer, antelope, jackrabbit and cottontail. These are the animals which that young man (the patient in the ceremonial) is hunting. In the opening (at the east) are Bat, Big Messenger Fly and Yellow Bird Messenger. First to fifth day (series).

[4]This statement is ambiguous. Perhaps it was meant to indicate some sort of identity or pairing of the Black and Yellow Talking-gods, and of the Blue and White Talking-gods.

Bibliography

Aberle, David F.
   1966   *The Peyote Religion Among the Navaho.* Chicago: Aldine
          Publishing Company.

Bailey, Lynn R.
   1970   *Bosque Redondo: An American Concentration Camp.*
          Pasadena: Socio-Technical Books.

Courlander, Harold
   1971   *The Fourth World of the Hopis.* Greenwich, Conn.:
          Fawcett Publications.

Cushing, Frank H.
   1920   *Zuni Breadstuff.* New York: Museum of the American
          Indian, Heye Foundation.

Dobie, J. Frank
   1961   *The Voice of the Coyote.* Lincoln: University of Nebraska
          Press.

Dozier, Edward P.
   1970   *The Pueblo Indians of North America.* New York: Holt,
          Rinehart, Winston.

Dutton, Bertha
   1974   *Indians of the American Southwest.* Englewood Cliffs:
          Prentice Hall.

Fewkes, Jesse Walter
   1898   "Tusayan Migration Traditions," *BAE Annual Report* 19.
   1903   "Hopi Katcinas Drawn by Native Artists," *BAE Annual
          Report* 21.

Franciscan Fathers
   1910   *An Ethnologic Dictionary of the Navajo Language.* St.
          Michaels, Arizona: St. Michaels Press.

Gladwin, Harold S.
   1957   *A History of the Ancient Southwest.* Portland: Bond Wheel-
          wright.

Goossen, Irvy W.
  1968   *Navajo Made Easier.* Flagstaff: Northland Press.
Haile, Father Berard
  1942   "Navaho Upward-Reaching Way and Emergence Place,"
          American Anthropologist 44, 407-20.
  1943   "Soul Concepts of the Navaho," *Annali Lateranensi* 7.
  1946   *The Navaho War Dance.* St. Michaels, Arizona: St.
          Michaels Press.
  ⌐ 1947 *Head and Face Masks in Navaho Ceremonialism.* St.
          Michaels, Arizona: St. Michaels Press.
  1950   *Legend of the Ghostway Ritual in the Male Branch of
          Shootingway—Suckingway, its Legend and Practice.*
          St. Michaels, Arizona: St. Michaels Press.
  1978   *Love-magic and Butterfly People, the Slim Curly Version
          of the Ajiłee and Mothway Myths.* American Tribal Reli-
          gions series, vol. 2. Flagstaff: The Museum of Northern
          Arizona Press.
Hill, W.W.
  1938   *The Agricultural and Hunting Methods of the Navaho
          Indians.* Yale University Publications in Anthropology,
          vol. 18.
Hill, W.W. and D.W. Hill
  ⌐ 1943 "The Myth of the Coyote Chantway," *New Mexico Anthro-
          pologist,* vol. 5, 6-8, no. 3, 111-13.
  ⌐ 1945 "Navaho Coyote Tales and Their Position in the Southern
          Athapaskan Group," *Journal of American Folklore,* vol. 58.
Kelly, Laurence C.
  1970   *Navajo Roundup.* Boulder, Colorado: Pruett Press.
Kewanwytewa, J.
  1961   "Legend of the Snake Clan," unpublished manuscript at the
          Museum of Northern Arizona.
Kluckhohn, Clyde
  1944   *Navaho Witchcraft.* Boston: Beacon Press.
Kluckhohn, Clyde and Dorothea Leighton
  1962   *The Navaho.* (Originally published in 1946.) Garden City:
          Doubleday—the American Museum of Natural History.
Kluckhohn, Clyde and Leland C. Wyman
  1940   "An Introduction to Navaho Chant Practice," *Memoirs of
          the American Anthropological Association* 53.
Ladd, E.
  1960   "Zuni Ethno-ornitology," unpublished master's thesis, the
          University of New Mexico.

Levy, Jerrold E.
1963   *Navajo Health Concepts and Behavior.* Window Rock: U.S. Public Health Service.

Luckert, Karl W.
1975   *The Navajo Hunter Tradition.* Tucson: The University of Arizona Press.
1976   *Olmec Religion, a Key to Middle America and Beyond.* Norman: The University of Oklahoma Press.
1977   *Navajo Mountain and Rainbow Bridge Religion.* American Tribal Religions series, vol. 1. Flagstaff: The Museum of Northern Arizona Press.
1978   *A Navajo Bringing-Home Ceremony, the Claus Chee Sonny Version of Deerway* Ajiłee. American Tribal Religions series, vol. 3. Flagstaff: The Museum of Northern Arizona Press.

McGregor, John C.
1965   *Southwestern Archaeology.* Second edition. Urbana: The University of Illinois Press.

Matthews, Washington
1887   "The Mountain Chant," *BAE Annual Report* 5.
1897   *Navaho Legends.* Boston: Houghton, Mifflin and Company.
1902   *The Night Chant, a Navaho Ceremony.* New York: Museum of Natural History.

Morgan, William
1936   "Human Wolves Among the Navaho," *Yale University Publications in Anthropology*, vol. 11.

Nequatewa, Edmund
1967   *Truth of a Hopi.* Flagstaff: Museum of Northern Arizona.

Newcomb, Franc
1940   "Origin Legend of the Navaho Eagle Chant," *Journal of American Folklore*, vol. 53.

Olin, Caroline B.
1972   *Navajo Indian Sandpainting; the Construction of Symbols.* Ph.D. dissertation, University of Stockholm.

Opler, Morris E.
1940   *Myths and Legends of the Lipan Apache Indians.* New York: American Folklore Society.
1943   "The Character and Derivation of the Jicarilla Holiness Rites," *The University of New Mexico Bulletin, Anthropological Series*, vol. 4, no. 3.
1965   *An Apache Lifeway.* New York: Cooper Square Publishers.

Parsons, Elsie C.
    1939   *Pueblo Religion.* 2 vols. Chicago: The University of
           Chicago Press.
    1940   "Taos Tales," *Memoirs of the American Folklore Society,*
           vol. 34.
Reichard, Gladys A.
    1950   *Navaho Religion, a Study of Symbolism.* 2 vols. New York:
           Bollingen Foundation.
    no date "The Chant of Waning Endurance," unpublished manu-
           script at the Museum of Northern Arizona.
Spencer, Katherine
    1947   Reflection of Social Life in the Navaho Origin Myth.
           University of New Mexico Publications in Anthropology,
           vol. 3.
    1957   Mythology and Values: An Analysis of Navaho Chantway
           Myths. *Memoirs of the American Folklore Society* 48.
Spicer, Edward
    1962   *Cycles of Conquest.* Tucson: University of Arizona Press.
Stephen, Alexander M.
    1936   *Hopi Journal.* Elsie C. Parsons, ed. 2 vols. New York:
           Columbia University Press.
Terrell, John U.
    1970   *The Navajos.* New York: Harper and Row.
Tozzer, A.M.
    1909   *Notes on Religious Ceremonies of the Navaho.* Cedar
           Rapids, Iowa.
Tyler, Hamilton A.
    1964   *Pueblo Gods and Myths.* Norman: University of Oklahoma
           Press.
    1975   *Pueblo Animals and Myths.* Norman: University of Okla-
           homa Press.
Underhill, Ruth M.
    1948   *Ceremonial Patterns in the Greater Southwest.* New York:
           American Ethnological Society.
    1954   "Intercultural Relations in the Greater Southwest," *Ameri-
           can Anthropologist,* vol. 56.
    1956   *The Navajos.* Norman: University of Oklahoma Press.
Waters, Frank
    1963   *Book of the Hopi.* New York: Viking Press.

Wheelwright, Mary C.
  1949   *Emergence Myth according to the Hanelthnayhe or Upwardreaching Rite.* Santa Fe: Museum of Navaho Ceremonial Art.
  1950   "Notes on Some Navaho Coyote Myths," *New Mexico Folklore Record*, vol. 4.
  1956   *The Myths and Prayers of the Great Star Chant and the Myth of the Coyote Chant.* Santa Fe: Museum of Navaho Ceremonial Art.
Wheelwright, Mary and Hasteen Klah.
  1942   *Navajo Creation Myth—the Story of Emergence.* Santa Fe: Museum of Navaho Ceremonial Art.
Wyman, Leland C.
  1950   "The Religion of the Navaho Indians," in *Forgotten Religions*, V. Ferm, ed. New York: Philosophical Library.
  1951   "Notes on Obsolete Navaho Ceremonies," *Plateau*, vol. 23, no. 3. Flagstaff: Museum of Northern Arizona.
  1962   *The Windways of the Navaho.* Colorado Springs: Taylor Museum.
  1965   *The Red Antway of the Navaho.* Santa Fe: Museum of Navaho Ceremonial Art.
  1970a *Blessingway.* Tucson: University of Arizona Press.
  1970b *Sandpaintings of the Navaho Shootingway and the Walcott Collection.* Washington, D.C.: Smithsonian Institution.
Wyman, Leland C. and S.K. Harris
  1941   "Navajo Indian Medical Ethnobotany," *The University of New Mexico Bulletin*, vol. 3, no. 5.
Wyman, Leland C., W.W. Hill and Iva Osanai
  1942   "Navaho Eschatology," *University of New Mexico Bulletin* 377. Albuquerque.
Wyman, Leland C. and Clyde Kluckhohn
  1938   "Navaho Classification of their Song Ceremonials." *Memoirs of the Anthropological Association* 50.
Young, Robert W.
  1968   *The Role of the Navaho in the Southwestern Drama.* Gallup, New Mexico.
Young, Robert W. and William Morgan
  1972   *The Navajo Language.* Salt Lake City: Deseret Book Company.

Index

Adulterous Coyote: 83, 103, 104, 127, 204
Ajiłee (Excessway): 6, 228; Coyoteway
    used for sexual misbehavior, 231
Armer, Laura: 16, 126, 203, 225-28

Badger foot: 139, 141, 142, 182
Basket-drum: 25, 96, 97-120, 183, 185,
    186
Begochidi: 4
Big Mustache: *see* Many Whiskers
Bit'ahnii Bidághaaí: 228-30
Black-god: 4
Blessing songs: 97-120, 185
Blessingway: 10, 139
Blood: 77-78, 82, 100-101
Burning the Feathers: 16, 20, 22 n, 48-52,
    87, 117-20, 153, 181, 204

Calling-god: 4, 69, 115-17, 123, 124, 128,
    203
Charlie, William: 6 n, 8, 217-23, 230-33
Cigarette: *see* Reed-prayerstick
Cook, Luke: ix, xi-xv, 6, 8, 9, 16, 18, 20,
    21, 25, 122, 129, 131, 135, 204
Cooke, Johnny: ix, xi-xiv, 21, 25
Corn (maize): 97, 122, 127, 133, 137,
    139, 146, 159, 160, 180
Cornmeal: 5, 88, 93, 117, 144
Cornmeal circle: 34, 35

Coyote (directional, animal and cosmic
    forms): 6, 7, 8, 9, 11, 18, 22 n, 45,
    50-52, 60, 65, 67, 69, 70, 75-76, 81,
    107-11, 126, 127, 135
Coyote Carrier: 122, 125, 167, 170, 171,
    172, 174, 176, 178
Coyote clan: 15, 18, 191
Coyote fur (skin): 75-77, 86, 112, 128;
    Hogan as fur, 100, 112
Coyote Girl: 69, 126, 127, 129, 130, 135,
    137, 142, 160, 163, 172, 179, 188,
    225, 226, 227
Coyote illness: 8, 9, 127
Coyoteway: classification of, 5-6; myth,
    18-19, 20-22, 133, 159, 191-202, 203-
    216, 217-23; recording of, ix, xi-xv;
    ritual sequence, 7, 8, 25-30; singers,
    ix, xii-xiv, 15-22, 191, 203, 217;
    theology, 126-29

Defamation, of gods: 10, 187

Eliade, Mircea: 12
Emergence, emergence hole: 4, 10 n5, 18,
    20, 103, 130, 132, 133, 137, 140,
    143, 146, 180, 218; birth of human-
    kind, 149; shamanic descent, 148-49;
    see also Underworld
Eschatology: 10 n5

Reed-prayerstick: 59, 201, 202; bundle, 53, 54-73, 164, 181, 182, 230; delivery of bundle, 70-73, 182
Ross, H.D.: 231

Underworld, underground: 4, 7, 10 n5, 18, 19, 20, 34, 50, 97, 104, 129, 133, 135, 142, 144, 146, 191, 192, 203; *see also* Emergence
Unraveling: 25, 26, 31-52, 87, 118, 130
Upwardreachingway: 11, 22 n, 204

Sandpainting: 25, 129-41, 159; carried away, 182-83
Shaman, shamanism: 3, 4, 5, 12, 13, 94, 127, 129, 135, 142, 146, 148, 191, 192, 218; shamanic descent, *see* Emergence hole
Singer: ix, xii-xiv, 3, 12, 192; initiation of, xiii-xv, 9, 34, 50, 186
Sliding lizards: 101, 127, 204
Smoking: *see* Reed-prayerstick
Spruce twigs: 74, 87, 89, 160, 167
Sweating: 48, 49, 53, 73-87, 128, 232

Washing: 53, 87-96
Water Serpent: 19 n, 192
Weapon- or Fightingway *(deezláji):* 10, 11
Wheelwright, Mary: 124, 191, 203, 224, 229
Witchcraft, witches: 9, 10 n4, 16, 22 n, 59, 86, 88, 117, 127, 204; for counter-witchcraft measures *see* Burning the Feathers *and* Sweating
Woodmann, Pierre: 229
Wooltáád bundle, Unraveling bundle: 31-33, 42-45, 60, 87, 201, 202
Wyman, Leland: 5, 6, 12, 128
Wyman, Leland and Clyde Kluckhohn: 9

Talking-god *(yé'iibicheii),* grandfather of the gods: 4, 69, 115-17, 121-25, 128, 129, 135, 137, 159, 160, 163, 167, 179, 180, 203, 233 n; his cosmic dimension, 188; impersonated, 165, 166, 167, 169, 170, 172, 173, 174, 175, 177
Tobacco, use of: *see* Reed-prayerstick
Trickster: 10, 10 n3, 11, 218
Tséyi'nii: 124, 127, 159, 203-16

Yellow Hair: 16
Yellow Man of the Canyon People: 18
Yoo'Hataałii: 124, 126, 191-202
Yucca: 87, 89, 90, 91, 97, 98

Zaa'nił (medicine to drink): 45-46, 139, 141, 142, 146, 149, 150, 180
Zuni: 8, 22 n, 48 n